IN ASSOCIATION WITH

SQA

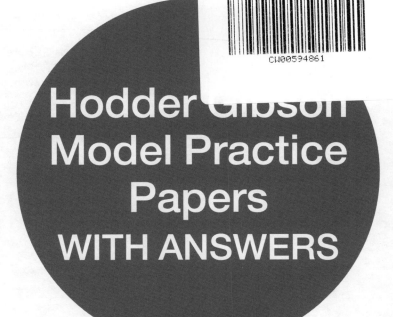

Hodder Gibson Model Practice Papers WITH ANSWERS

PLUS: Official SQA Specimen Paper With Answers

Higher for CfE
Spanish

2014 Specimen Question Paper & Model Papers

HODDER GIBSON
AN HACHETTE UK COMPANY

This book contains the official 2014 SQA Specimen Question Paper for Higher for CfE Spanish, with associated SQA approved answers modified from the official marking instructions that accompany the paper.

In addition the book contains model practice papers, together with answers, plus study skills advice. These papers, some of which may include a limited number of previously published SQA questions, have been specially commissioned by Hodder Gibson, and have been written by experienced senior teachers and examiners in line with the new Higher for CfE syllabus and assessment outlines, Spring 2014. This is not SQA material but has been devised to provide further practice for Higher for CfE examinations in 2015 and beyond.

Hodder Gibson is grateful to the copyright holders, as credited on the final page of the Answer Section, for permission to use their material. Every effort has been made to trace the copyright holders and to obtain their permission for the use of copyright material. Hodder Gibson will be happy to receive information allowing us to rectify any error or omission in future editions.

Hachette UK's policy is to use papers that are natural, renewable and recyclable products and made from wood grown in sustainable forests. The logging and manufacturing processes are expected to conform to the environmental regulations of the country of origin.

Orders: please contact Bookpoint Ltd, 130 Park Drive, Abingdon, Oxon OX14 4SE. Telephone: (44) 01235 827720. Fax: (44) 01235 400454. Lines are open 9.00–5.00, Monday to Saturday, with a 24-hour message answering service. Visit our website at www.hoddereducation.co.uk. Hodder Gibson can be contacted direct on: Tel: 0141 848 1609; Fax: 0141 889 6315; email: hoddergibson@hodder.co.uk

This collection first published in 2015 by
Hodder Gibson, an imprint of Hodder Education,
An Hachette UK Company
2a Christie Street
Paisley PA1 1NB

BrightRED   Hodder Gibson is grateful to Bright Red Publishing Ltd for collaborative work in preparation of this book and all SQA Past Paper,
PUBLISHING   National 5 and Higher for CfE Model Paper titles 2014.

Typeset by PDQ Digital Media Solutions Ltd, Bungay, Suffolk NR35 1BY

Printed in the UK

A catalogue record for this title is available from the British Library

ISBN: 978-1-4718-3999-3

3 2 1

2016 2015

Introduction

Study Skills – what you need to know to pass exams!

Pause for thought

Many students might skip quickly through a page like this. After all, we all know how to revise. Do you really though?

Think about this:

"IF YOU ALWAYS DO WHAT YOU ALWAYS DO, YOU WILL ALWAYS GET WHAT YOU HAVE ALWAYS GOT."

Do you like the grades you get? Do you want to do better? If you get full marks in your assessment, then that's great! Change nothing! This section is just to help you get that little bit better than you already are.

There are two main parts to the advice on offer here. The first part highlights fairly obvious things but which are also very important. The second part makes suggestions about revision that you might not have thought about but which WILL help you.

Part 1

DOH! It's so obvious but …

Start revising in good time

Don't leave it until the last minute – this will make you panic.

Make a revision timetable that sets out work time AND play time.

Sleep and eat!

Obvious really, and very helpful. Avoid arguments or stressful things too – even games that wind you up. You need to be fit, awake and focused!

Know your place!

Make sure you know exactly **WHEN and WHERE** your exams are.

Know your enemy!

Make sure you know what to expect in the exam.

How is the paper structured?

How much time is there for each question?

What types of question are involved?

Which topics seem to come up time and time again?

Which topics are your strongest and which are your weakest?

Are all topics compulsory or are there choices?

Learn by DOING!

There is no substitute for past papers and practice papers – they are simply essential! Tackling this collection of papers and answers is exactly the right thing to be doing as your exams approach.

Part 2

People learn in different ways. Some like low light, some bright. Some like early morning, some like evening/night. Some prefer warm, some prefer cold. But everyone uses their BRAIN and the brain works when it is active. Passive learning – sitting gazing at notes – is the most INEFFICIENT way to learn anything. Below you will find tips and ideas for making your revision more effective and maybe even more enjoyable. What follows gets your brain active, and active learning works!

Activity 1 – Stop and review

Step 1

When you have done no more than 5 minutes of revision reading STOP!

Step 2

Write a heading in your own words which sums up the topic you have been revising.

Step 3

Write a summary of what you have revised in no more than two sentences. Don't fool yourself by saying, "I know it, but I cannot put it into words". That just means you don't know it well enough. If you cannot write your summary, revise that section again, knowing that you must write a summary at the end of it. Many of you will have notebooks full of blue/black ink writing. Many of the pages will not be especially attractive or memorable so try to liven them up a bit with colour as you are reviewing and rewriting. **This is a great memory aid, and memory is the most important thing.**

Activity 2 – Use technology!

Why should everything be written down? Have you thought about "mental" maps, diagrams, cartoons and colour to help you learn? And rather than write down notes, why not record your revision material?

What about having a text message revision session with friends? Keep in touch with them to find out how and what they are revising and share ideas and questions.

Why not make a video diary where you tell the camera what you are doing, what you think you have learned and what you still have to do? No one has to see or hear it, but the process of having to organise your thoughts in a formal way to explain something is a very important learning practice.

Be sure to make use of electronic files. You could begin to summarise your class notes. Your typing might be slow, but it will get faster and the typed notes will be easier to read than the scribbles in your class notes. Try to add different fonts and colours to make your work stand out. You can easily Google relevant pictures, cartoons and diagrams which you can copy and paste to make your work more attractive and **MEMORABLE**.

Activity 3 – This is it. Do this and you will know lots!

Step 1

In this task you must be very honest with yourself! Find the SQA syllabus for your subject (www.sqa.org.uk). Look at how it is broken down into main topics called MANDATORY knowledge. That means stuff you MUST know.

Step 2

BEFORE you do ANY revision on this topic, write a list of everything that you already know about the subject. It might be quite a long list but you only need to write it once. It shows you all the information that is already in your long-term memory so you know what parts you do not need to revise!

Step 3

Pick a chapter or section from your book or revision notes. Choose a fairly large section or a whole chapter to get the most out of this activity.

With a buddy, use Skype, Facetime, Twitter or any other communication you have, to play the game "If this is the answer, what is the question?". For example, if you are revising Geography and the answer you provide is "meander", your buddy would have to make up a question like "What is the word that describes a feature of a river where it flows slowly and bends often from side to side?".

Make up 10 "answers" based on the content of the chapter or section you are using. Give this to your buddy to solve while you solve theirs.

Step 4

Construct a wordsearch of at least 10 X 10 squares. You can make it as big as you like but keep it realistic. Work together with a group of friends. Many apps allow you to make wordsearch puzzles online. The words and phrases can go in any direction and phrases can be split. Your puzzle must only contain facts linked to the topic you are revising. Your task is to find 10 bits of information to hide in your puzzle, but you must not repeat information that you used in Step 3. DO NOT show where the words are. Fill up empty squares with random letters. Remember to keep a note of where your answers are hidden but do not show your friends. When you have a complete puzzle, exchange it with a friend to solve each other's puzzle.

Step 5

Now make up 10 questions (not "answers" this time) based on the same chapter used in the previous two tasks. Again, you must find NEW information that you have not yet used. Now it's getting hard to find that new information! Again, give your questions to a friend to answer.

Step 6

As you have been doing the puzzles, your brain has been actively searching for new information. Now write a NEW LIST that contains only the new information you have discovered when doing the puzzles. Your new list is the one to look at repeatedly for short bursts over the next few days. Try to remember more and more of it without looking at it. After a few days, you should be able to add words from your second list to your first list as you increase the information in your long-term memory.

FINALLY! Be inspired...

Make a list of different revision ideas and beside each one write **THINGS I HAVE** tried, **THINGS I WILL** try and **THINGS I MIGHT** try. Don't be scared of trying something new.

And remember – "FAIL TO PREPARE AND PREPARE TO FAIL!"

Higher Spanish

The course

The Higher Spanish course aims to enable you to develop the ability to:

- read, listen, talk and write in Spanish
- understand and use Spanish
- apply your knowledge and understanding of the language.

The course offers the opportunity to develop detailed language skills in the real-life contexts of society, learning, employability, and culture.

How the course is graded

The course assessment will take the form of a performance and a written exam.

- The performance will be a presentation and discussion with your teacher, which will be recorded and marked by your teacher. This is out of 30, and makes up 30% of your final mark.
- The written exam will be sat in May. This book will help you practise for the exam.

The exams

Reading and Directed Writing

- Exam time: 1 hour 40 minutes

Reading

- Total marks: 30
- Weighting in final grade: 30%
- What you have to do: read a passage of about 600 words, and answer questions about it in English, including an overall purpose question for 20 marks; then translate an extract from the passage of about 40 words into English for 10 marks.

Directed Writing

- Total marks: 10
- Weighting in final grade: 10%
- What you have to do: write 120–150 words in Spanish describing a visit you made, or an experience you had, in a Spanish speaking country.

Listening and Personal Response Writing

- Exam time: 60 minutes
- Total marks: 30
- Weighting in final grade: 30%
- What you have to do: Section 1 (20 marks): listen to a presentation in Spanish, and answer questions in English for 8 marks; then listen to a conversation in Spanish, and answer questions about it in English for 12 marks; Section 2 (10 marks): write 120–150 words in Spanish as a personal response to the topic

discussed in the conversation: there will be three specific questions to be addressed.

How to improve your mark!

Reading

- Read the whole passage, then pick out the key points. Detailed answers are generally required, so pay particular attention to words like *tanto*, *muy*, *demasiado*, *un poco*, and to negatives. Make sure you get the details of numbers, days, times etc. right.
- Use the line numbers above each question to guide you as to where to look for the answer.
- Take care when using dictionaries where a word has more than one meaning. Learn to choose the correct meaning from a list of meanings in a dictionary, and get in the habit of going beyond the headword. Often you will find the whole phrase you are looking for further down the entry.
- Try to answer the specific wording of the question, but do not give a word-for-word translation of the text as a response to the reading comprehension questions, as this often results in an answer which is not in correct English.
- When responding to the questions in the Reading papers, you should be guided by the number of points awarded for each question. You should give as much detail in your answer as you have understood, but should not put down everything which is in the original text, as you are wasting time. The question itself usually indicates the amount of information required by stating in bold, e.g. "State **two** of them". If the question says "Give **any** two", there are more than two possibilities, so choose the two you are happiest with and stick to them.
- The final question before the translation asks you to look at the passage as a whole, then answer a question and provide evidence to back up your answer. It is important to start your answer with your opinion, then select pieces of text from the passage to back up your answer, giving an English version of what is in the passage.
- Look closely at each word in each section of the translation passage, and pay particular attention to the articles and tenses used. Make sure you include each word in your translation (although translation is not word for word!). Look at marking schemes for translations to give you an idea of what a good translation should look like.

Directed Writing

- Have a quick look at the two choices for writing, and go for the one for which your prepared material will give you most support.
- Consider, carefully, the wording of each bullet point, and make sure any learned material that you use is relevant and appropriate to the bullet point. Make sure you address each part of the first bullet point, and that you are answering the questions asked.
- Use your dictionary to check the accuracy of what you have written (spelling, genders etc.), but not to create and invent new sentences.
- Don't write pieces that are too long, you only need 120–150 words. So stick to 30–40 words per bullet point.
- Be aware of the extended criteria used in assessing performances in Writing (included in the Answer Section of this book!), so that you know what's required to achieve the good and very good categories in terms of content, accuracy, and range and variety of language.
- Ensure that your handwriting is legible (particularly when writing in Spanish) and distinguish clearly between rough notes and what you wish to be considered as your final answers. Make sure you score out your notes!
- You should bear in mind the following points:
  - There are four bullet points to answer: they are not really predictable and vary from year to year, but certain things come up regularly.
  - Each of the four bullet points should have between 30 and 40 words to address it properly.
  - You will be assessed on how well you have answered the points, and on the accuracy of your language.
  - If you miss out or fail to address a bullet point correctly, the most you can get is six marks.
  - For a mark of good or very good, you should use some complex language such as longer, varied sentences, adjectives and conjunctions.

Listening

- Your listening skills will improve most with practice. So use the Listening sections in this book several times to get used to the format of the exam.
- Read the questions carefully before the first listening and use them as a means of anticipating the sort of information you will need to extract from the text.
- Not giving enough detail is still a major reason for candidates losing marks. Many answers are correct as far as they go, but don't have enough detail to score marks. The same rules as for Reading apply. Give as much detail as possible in your answers and don't lose marks by writing down numbers, prepositions and question words inaccurately.
- You hear each of the two Listening texts twice only, so make use of the gap between the two recordings to check which specific details you still need for your answers, so your listening is focused.
- Make sure you're able to give accurate answers through confident knowledge of numbers, common adjectives, weather expressions, prepositions and question words, so that some of the "easier" points of information are not lost through lack of sufficiently accurate details.
- When responding to the questions in the Listening papers, be guided by the number of points awarded for each question, and by the wording of the question. You should give as much detail in your answer as you have understood, but should not write down everything you hear. The question itself usually indicates the amount of information required by stating in bold, e.g. "Give **2** of them".
- Be sure to put a line through any notes you have made!

Personal Response Writing

- Make sure you read the stimulus questions carefully and adapt any learned material you use so it's relevant to the aspects contained in them.
- There are three questions to be answered, and you must answer them all, at roughly the same length. Aim for 40 to 50 words for each of them.
- Don't be tempted to rewrite an answer you have written on the topic previously: you have to be sure your answer is relevant to the questions put to you.

Good luck!

Remember that the rewards for passing Higher Spanish are well worth it! Your pass will help you get the future you want for yourself. In the exam, be confident in your own ability. If you're not sure how to answer a question, trust your instincts and just give it a go anyway – keep calm and don't panic! GOOD LUCK!

HIGHER FOR CfE

2014 Specimen Question Paper

National Qualifications SPECIMEN ONLY

SQ42/H/11

Spanish Reading

Date — Not applicable

Duration — 1 hour and 40 minutes

Total marks — 30

Attempt ALL questions.

Write your answers clearly, in **English**, in the Reading Answer Booklet provided. In the answer booklet you must clearly identify the question number you are attempting.

You may use a Spanish dictionary.

Use **blue** or **black** ink.

There is a separate question and answer booklet for Directed Writing. You must complete your answer for Directed Writing in the question and answer booklet for Directed Writing.

Before leaving the examination room you must give your Reading answer booklet and your Directed Writing question and answer booklet to the Invigilator; if you do not, you may lose all the marks for this paper.

Total marks — 30

This Reading Paper replaces the original one in the SQA Specimen Paper, which cannot be reproduced for copyright reasons. As such, it should be stressed that it is not an official SQA verified section, although every care has been taken by the Publishers to ensure that it offers appropriate practice material for CfE Higher.

Read the whole article carefully and then answer, in English, ALL the questions that follow.

The article discusses the impact of the digital age.

Significado de Era digital

¿Qué es la Era Digital? La Era Digital, también conocida como Era de la Información y de las Telecomunicaciones es, simplemente, el mundo en el que vivimos actualmente. Esta etapa comenzó cuando se inventó el teléfono, pero la mayor revolución ha sido, sin lugar a dudas, la invención de Internet. La Era Digital es diferente de las etapas anteriores de
5 la Historia, porque ahora la mayoría de la gente puede acceder a cualquier tipo de información de forma muy rápida y barata.

Con la revolución digital podemos hacer casi todo en Internet con un clic del ratón de nuestro ordenador: comprar comida, reservar una habitación de hotel, leer el periódico, ver la televisión, comunicarnos con nuestros amigos... Cada vez existen más y más
10 aplicaciones y programas que hacen nuestra vida más fácil.

También en el trabajo, ha ocurrido toda una revolución. Cada vez en más y más países, el trabajo se hace más fácil y rápido gracias a numerosos programas. Por ejemplo, antes había que escribir un texto a máquina (¡o incluso a mano!), fotocopiarlo y mandarlo por carta o por fax. Sin embargo, ahora se escribe directamente en el ordenador, se pueden
15 incluir gráficos, imágenes, etcétera y luego mandar el documento por correo electrónico. ¡Ahora podemos hacer todo esto incluso utilizando el teléfono móvil! Gracias a esto, los trabajos se van haciendo poco a poco más flexibles y cada vez existen más personas que trabajan desde casa. Sin embargo, no hay que olvidar que no todas las personas tienen acceso a la tecnología de la misma forma. En muchos países del Tercer Mundo, las
20 personas carecen de medios económicos suficientes para comprar un ordenador o un teléfono móvil de última generación, o pagar la cuota de Internet.

Hay muchísimas consecuencias positivas derivadas de las nuevas tecnologías de la comunicación, sin embargo, aquí queremos destacar una: el acceso a la información. En el mundo moderno y gracias a la tecnología, tenemos acceso a todo tipo de información
25 con solo hacer clic en Internet y buscar en un motor de búsqueda como Google. La mayoría de los periódicos y publicaciones se encuentran ya en también en Internet y actualizan la información constantemente. Incluso las noticias que no aparecen en los periódicos, a causa de que no hay espacio suficiente, suelen encontrarse sin problema en Internet, porque allí no hay limitación de espacio físico.

30 Por supuesto, en la Era Digital no todo es de color de rosa, sino que también encontramos personas que utilizan las nuevas tecnologías para causar daño o sufrimiento, comunicar ideas negativas. Por ejemplo, personas que, en su tiempo libre, dejan comentarios en artículos o videos de Internet que atacan personalmente al autor y que solo buscan causar sufrimiento, sin hacer ninguna crítica constructiva.

35 Otro problema podemos observar es que, en algunos casos, la tecnología nos impide apreciar a las personas y los paisajes que nos rodean, pues estamos más preocupados de ver si tenemos un correo electrónico nuevo o si alguien nos ha dejado un comentario en las redes sociales.

En general, podemos decir que los avances en las tecnologías digitales hacen nuestra vida
40 mucho más fácil, nos conectan con el mundo y con personas que están lejos. Sin embargo,
no debemos olvidar prestar atención a las personas que tenemos a nuestro lado.

MARKS

Questions

Re-read lines 1—6

1. In what way does the article define the digital era?   1

2. What two inventions started the digital age?   1

3. What is different about the digital age? Give details.   2

Re-read lines 7—10

4. In what way do we access data, according to the article?   1

5. State any three things we can now do, according to the article.   3

Re-read lines 14—21

6. What have been two effects of the new era?   2

7. Which people may not have full access to the new era?   1

Re-read lines 24—29

8. What use do newspapers make of new technologies?   1

9. What advantage does the internet hold for newspapers?   1

Re-read lines 35—41

10. What negative effects of the new era does the article note? Give details.   3

11. What might stop us appreciating the people and places we come across?   2

12. Now consider the article as a whole. Does the author give positive, negative or
    balanced view of the impact of new technologies? Justify your answer with
    reference to the text.   2

13. Translate into English lines 11—14. (También....fax)   10

[END OF SPECIMEN QUESTION PAPER]

H
National Qualifications
SPECIMEN ONLY

Mark

SQ42/H/02

Spanish
Directed Writing

Date — Not applicable

Duration — 1 hour and 40 minutes

Fill in these boxes and read what is printed below.

Full name of centre

Town

Forename(s)

Surname

Number of seat

Date of birth

Day   Month   Year

Scottish candidate number

Total marks — 10

Choose ONE scenario on *Page two* and write your answer clearly, in **Spanish**, in the space provided in this booklet. You must clearly identify the scenario number you are attempting.

You may use a Spanish dictionary.

Additional space for answers is provided at the end of this booklet.

Use **blue** or **black** ink.

There is a separate answer booklet for Reading. You must complete your answers for Reading in the answer booklet for Reading.

Before leaving the examination room you must give this Directed Writing question and answer booklet and your Reading answer booklet to the Invigilator; if you do not, you may lose all the marks for this paper.

Total marks — 10

Choose **one** of the following two scenarios.

SCENARIO 1: Employability

> Last summer, you spent a month working in Spain.
>
> You have been asked to write a report in Spanish for your school/college language webpage about your experience.

You must include the following information and **you should try to add** other relevant details:

- Where you worked **and** how you got the job

- What you had to do every day

- If you got on with your boss and the other employees

- If you would recommend working abroad

You should write approximately 120—150 words.

OR

SCENARIO 2: Culture

> While in Spain/Latin America, you attended a party organised by your Spanish/Latin American friend.
>
> You have been asked to write about your experience in Spanish for the language section of your school/college website.

You must include the following information and **you should try to add** other relevant details:

- Where you went **and** the reason your friend was having a party

- What the people were like that you met at the party

- What you enjoyed most about the party

- What plans you will make if your Spanish friend comes to visit you

You should write approximately 120—150 words.

ANSWER SPACE

MARKS | DO NOT WRITE IN THIS MARGIN

Scenario number

MARKS DO NOT WRITE IN THIS MARGIN

ANSWER SPACE (continued)

ANSWER SPACE (continued)

MARKS DO NOT WRITE IN THIS MARGIN

ANSWER SPACE (continued)

[END OF SPECIMEN QUESTION PAPER]

ADDITIONAL SPACE FOR ANSWERS

MARKS | DO NOT WRITE IN THIS MARGIN

MARKS | DO NOT WRITE IN THIS MARGIN

ADDITIONAL SPACE FOR ANSWERS

H

National Qualifications
SPECIMEN ONLY

Mark

SQ42/H/03

Spanish
Listening and Writing

Date — Not applicable

Duration — 1 hour

Fill in these boxes and read what is printed below.

Full name of centre

Town

Forename(s)

Surname

Number of seat

Date of birth

Day   Month   Year

Scottish candidate number

Total marks — 30

SECTION 1 — LISTENING — 20 marks

You will hear two items in Spanish. **Before you hear each item, you will have one minute to study the questions.** You will hear each item twice, with an interval of one minute between playings. You will then have time to answer the questions before hearing the next item. Write your answers clearly, in **English**, in the spaces provided.

SECTION 2 — WRITING — 10 marks

Write your answer clearly, in **Spanish**, in the space provided.

Attempt ALL questions. You may use a Spanish dictionary.

Additional space for answers is provided at the end of this booklet. If you use this space you must clearly identify the question number you are attempting.

You are not allowed to leave the examination room until the end of the test.

Use **blue** or **black** ink.

Before leaving the examination room you must give this booklet to the Invigilator; if you do not, you may lose all the marks for this paper.

MARKS | DO NOT WRITE IN THIS MARGIN

SECTION 1 — LISTENING — 20 marks
Attempt ALL questions

Item 1

You listen to Manuel, who talks about his leisure activities.

(a) (i) Why did Manuel stop playing football?   1

_____

(ii) In what ways does he stay involved in football? Give any **one** detail.   1

_____

(b) Manuel's passion for music started when he was very young. Give any **one** example.   1

_____

(c) What did Manuel discover in music? Give any **one** detail.   1

_____

(d) Manuel talks about a leisure survey.

(i) What are the two most common leisure activities amongst Spanish young people?   2

_____

_____

(ii) What surprises Manuel about the results of the survey?   1

_____

(e) Overall, which statement best describes Manuel's feelings about his leisure activities? Tick (✓) the correct statement.   1

His leisure activities are identical to those of typical young Spaniards.	
Leisure activities are important to him.	
He hasn't got enough time for his leisure activities.	

MARKS | DO NOT WRITE IN THIS MARGIN

Item 2

You listen to an online interview with a Spanish pop singer, Carmen.

(a) Carmen describes how her professional career started. Give any **two** details about this.

2

_____

_____

(b) Carmen has made the list of "People" magazine's 100 Most Beautiful. What does Carmen think about this? State any **one** thing.

1

_____

(c) Carmen talks about the advantages and disadvantages of being famous.

(i) State any **one** advantage.

1

_____

(ii) State any **one** disadvantage.

1

_____

(d) Carmen then talks about what makes her happy.

(i) What makes Carmen happy?

1

_____

(ii) She also loves to go back home. Why is this? Give any **one** reason.

1

_____

(e) When does Carmen find inspiration?

1

_____

(f) Apart from sport, what does Carmen do to stay healthy? Give any **two** details.

2

_____

_____

MARKS DO NOT WRITE IN THIS MARGIN

Item 2 (continued)

   (g) Finally, what does Carmen say about languages?　Give any **two** details.

          2

_____

_____

MARKS | DO NOT WRITE IN THIS MARGIN

SECTION 2 — WRITING — 10 marks

Carmen ha hablado de sus pasatiempos y de lo que hace para mantenerse en forma. Y tú, ¿qué haces para estar en forma? ¿Tienes muchos pasatiempos? ¿Crees que es importante tener pasatiempos sanos?

Escribe 120—150 palabras, en español, para expresar tus ideas.

ANSWER SPACE FOR SECTION 2 (continued)

[END OF SPECIMEN QUESTION PAPER]

ADDITIONAL SPACE FOR ANSWERS

MARKS

DO NOT
WRITE IN
THIS
MARGIN

ADDITIONAL SPACE FOR ANSWERS

National Qualifications
SPECIMEN ONLY

SQ42/H/13

Spanish
Listening Transcript

Date — Not applicable

Duration — 1 hour

This paper must not be seen by any candidate.

The material overleaf is provided for use in an emergency only (eg the recording or equipment proving faulty) or where permission has been given in advance by SQA for the material to be read to candidates with additional support needs. The material must be read exactly as printed.

Transcript — Higher

Instructions to reader(s):

For each item, read the English **once**, then read the Spanish **twice**, with an interval of 1 minute between the two readings. On completion of the second reading, pause for the length of time indicated in brackets after the item, to allow the candidates to write their answers.

Where special arrangements have been agreed in advance to allow the reading of the material, those sections marked **(f)** should be read by a female speaker and those marked **(m)** by a male; those sections marked **(t)** should be read by the teacher.

(t)   **Item 1**

You listen to Manuel who talks about his leisure activities.

You now have one minute to study the questions for Item 1.

(m)   En mi vida tengo dos pasiones, el deporte y la música:

Cuando tenía diez años empecé a jugar al fútbol con mis amigos del barrio. Cada día pasábamos muchas horas juntos en el parque entrenando. Yo era muy buen jugador, y me hubiera gustado ser futbolista profesional. Pero, con doce años empecé a tener problemas con la rodilla y no pude continuar jugando al fútbol, así que dejé de jugar al fútbol. A pesar del problema con la rodilla, para mí, el fútbol sigue siendo importante aunque ahora lo disfruto como espectador. Soy abonado de mi equipo favorito y no me pierdo nunca los partidos. También soy el asistente del entrenador de un equipo de niños pequeños.

Mi pasión por la música me viene desde que era muy joven: por ejemplo, con solo cinco años aprendí a tocar la guitarra, y cuando estaba en la escuela en vez de estudiar escribía canciones. Descubrí que la música era mi forma de expresarme, y una manera de olvidarme de los problemas. Estoy en un grupo de música pop con mis amigos y solemos ensayar casi todos los fines de semana.

La semana pasada leímos una encuesta en el instituto sobre los pasatiempos más populares de los jóvenes españoles: El primero era participar en deportes de equipo, como el fútbol o el baloncesto. El segundo más popular era pasar tiempo hablando con los amigos en las redes sociales. Me sorprende que los jóvenes ahora pasen más tiempo en las redes sociales, chateando con sus amigos en internet, que hablando con sus amigos cara a cara.

(2 minutes)

(t) Item 2

You listen to an online interview with a Spanish pop singer, Carmen.

You now have one minute to study the questions for Item 2.

(m) Hola Carmen, es un placer tenerte aquí con nosotros, muchas gracias.

(f) El placer es mío.

(m) Carmen, ¡te has hecho famosa muy rápidamente!, cuéntanos cómo empezó tu carrera profesional.

(f) Bueno, yo empecé cantando en el sofá blanco de mi casa y puse los videos en las redes sociales. Por esto tengo que reconocer que las nuevas tecnologías han jugado un papel muy importante en mi carrera profesional.

(m) Carmen, según la revista "People" eres una de las cien personas más bellas del mundo. . ., ¿qué piensas sobre esto?

(f) Pues para decir la verdad no me importa en absoluto. Yo me dedico a escribir canciones, a tocar la guitarra, y a lo que más me gusta, a cantar.

(m) Dime Carmen, ¿te gusta ser famosa?

(f) Ser famosa tiene ventajas. Por ejemplo, si me reconocen en un restaurante, insisten que me siente en una de las mejores mesas. Por las calles mucha gente me sonríe o mis fans me piden un autógrafo. Por otro lado, es difícil escaparme, o no llamar la atención. ¡Me gustaría entrar en una tienda sin que los dependientes me reconozcan!

(m) Y ¿qué te hace feliz?

(f) Hay muchas cosas que me hacen feliz, como irme de vacaciones o descansar en la playa pero lo que me encanta es volver a mi casa, a mi tierra, a Málaga, porque echo mucho de menos la comida de mi madre y me gusta pasar tiempo con mi familia.

(m) Cuéntame, ¿cómo buscas la inspiración para tus canciones?

(f) Bueno, como Málaga está en la costa, busco la inspiración cuando doy un paseo por la playa. Además, como estoy muy ocupada, a veces me llega la inspiración incluso hasta en el gimnasio haciendo ejercicio o en clase de zumba.

(m) Ah, en el gimnasio. ¿Y además del deporte, que más haces para mantenerte en forma?

(f) Para mí la salud es muy importante, por ejemplo nunca he fumado. Yo tengo una dieta muy equilibrada, no como mucha grasa e intento dormir ocho horas al día.

(m) Y, para terminar ¿qué tal se te dan los idiomas?

(f) Bueno, hablo francés con fluidez, y en mis conciertos siempre canto una canción en francés Quiero mejorar mi nivel de inglés porque considero que los idiomas son muy importantes. También me gusta escuchar música en inglés.

(2 minutes)

(t) End of test.

Now look over your answers.

[END OF SPECIMEN TRANSCRIPT]

Page three

Model Paper 1

Whilst this Model Practice Paper has been specially commissioned by Hodder Gibson for use as practice for the Higher (for Curriculum for Excellence) exams, the key reference document remains the SQA Specimen Paper 2014.

HODDER
GIBSON
LEARN MORE

National
Qualifications
MODEL PAPER 1

**Spanish
Reading**

Duration — 1 hour and 40 minutes

Total marks — 30

Attempt ALL questions.

Write your answers clearly, in **English**, in the Reading Answer Booklet provided. In the answer booklet, you must clearly identify the question number you are attempting.

You may use a Spanish dictionary.

Use **blue** or **black** ink.

There is a separate question and answer booklet for Directed Writing. You must complete your answer for Directed Writing in the question and answer booklet for Directed Writing.

Before leaving the examination room you must give your Reading answer booklet and your Directed Writing question and answer booklet to the Invigilator; if you do not, you may lose all the marks for this paper.

Total marks — 30

Read the whole article carefully and then answer, in English, ALL the questions that follow.

The writer discusses bullying in Spanish schools.

El nuevo acoso escolar

Ayer se publicaron los resultados de un estudio sobre el acoso entre los adolescentes españoles, y parece que el 11% de los jóvenes de entre 12—18 años son acosados por sus compañeros de instituto. Cuando analizamos estos datos, podemos observar que el acoso físico no ha aumentado en los últimos años, sino que ahora hay más acoso psicológico. Una de
5 las causas del acoso psicológico es que los jóvenes utilizan las nuevas tecnologías para acosar a sus compañeros, sobre todo, usan las redes sociales. Ahora los acosadores escriben comentarios en las redes sociales para reírse o burlarse de sus víctimas y también animan a otros a que se burlen de esa persona.

Esta es, por ejemplo, la historia de Pedro (no es su nombre real, sino un nombre inventado
10 para proteger su identidad), de 14 años de edad. Un compañero empezó a acosarlo en su red social. "Dejaba comentarios insultándome o amenazándome", nos cuenta Pedro y continúa, "cuando decidí no admitirlo más como amigo, creó una cuenta con mi nombre y la utilizó para insultarme y también para insultar a otros chicos en mi nombre". Además, en el pasado, los acosadores eran gente que conocían en persona a ese chico o a esa chica, ahora pueden estar
15 incluso en institutos distintos y no conocerse personalmente. La psicóloga, Leticia Campos, nos explica: "Este tipo de acoso causa más dolor y trauma para las víctimas, porque en muchos casos es de una humillación pública. A veces, son acosados por personas que no conocen, pero que han visto sus fotos en las redes sociales".

Otra de las dificultades para las víctimas es que a veces los adultos, tanto los padres como los
20 profesores, piensan que la responsabilidad no es solo del acosador, sino que la víctima causa el acoso. Para estos adultos, la causa del acoso es que las víctimas hacen o dicen cosas que los diferencian del resto de sus compañeros. Por ejemplo, un chico que siempre está leyendo cómics o que lleva ropa muy diferente. En el caso de Pedro, él dice: "Los chicos que me acosaban siempre me llamaban gordo y al principio, mi madre me decía que si perdía peso,
25 dejarían de meterse conmigo. Pero cuando hablamos con mi profesora, ella dijo que ellos son los que tienen que cambiar y no yo". Leticia Campos comenta: "No podemos culpar a los alumnos. Ni el aspecto físico, ni la forma de ser ni de actuar son razones suficientes para acosar a una persona."

Sin embargo, otra característica más positiva es que el acoso cibernético es más fácil de
30 probar, porque se puede saber desde qué ordenador se escribió un mensaje, así como la hora y la fecha en la que se publicó. Así, los culpables pueden ser castigados y también reeducados para que comprendan que los insultos y las humillaciones tienen consecuencias muy negativas en la vida de otra persona.

Para concluir, ¿cuál es la solución a este problema? Todos los expertos están de acuerdo: la
35 solución es educación, educación y educación. Los jóvenes tienen que aprender la importancia del respeto a los demás. Cada año más institutos y colegios tienen cursos en los que un psicólogo o profesor explica a los alumnos qué es el acoso escolar y qué hacer cuando lo sufren o si conocen a alguna víctima. También es importante que los profesores y padres aprendan a actuar en los casos de acoso y, por último, hay que invitar a los jóvenes que sufren acoso a
40 decírselo a sus padres o profesores, para que no estén solos y para solucionar el problema.

MARKS

Questions

Re-read lines 1—8

1. The opening of the article discusses the publication of a recent study on bullying in Spanish schools.

    (a) What do we learn of the significance of the statistics?   1

    (b) Why does more psychological bullying now take place? Give any **two** details.   2

    (c) What do bullies now do which makes matters worse?   1

Re-read lines 9—16

2. We are given some specific examples of bullying.

    (a) In what way did Pedro's problems start? Give details.   2

    (b) In what way did things escalate? Give any **two** details.   2

    (c) What has changed over the last few years?   1

Re-read lines 19—28

3. The article gives advice on how teachers and parents might get involved.

    (a) What might cause the bullying? State any **two** things.   2

    (b) What **two** different reactions to his situation did Pedro's mother and teacher have?   2

Re-read lines 29—33

4. The author discusses cyber bullying. What positive aspect does the author note, and what can this result in?   2

Re-read lines 34—40

5. The author discusses possible solutions to the problem.

    (a) What are schools doing more and more? State **two** things.   2

    (b) What is it important for parents and teachers to do?   1

MARKS

6. Now consider the article as a whole. Does the author give the impression that bullying is so widespread it cannot properly be dealt with? Give details from the text to justify your answer.

2

7. Translate into English:

10

"Este ... sociales." (*lines 16—18*)

[END OF MODEL QUESTION PAPER]

National Qualifications
MODEL PAPER 1

Spanish
Directed Writing

Duration — 1 hour and 40 minutes

Fill in these boxes and read what is printed below.

Full name of centre

Town

Forename(s)

Surname

Number of seat

Date of birth
Day   Month   Year

Scottish candidate number

Total marks — 10

Choose ONE scenario on *Page two* and write your answer clearly, in **Spanish**, in the space provided in this booklet. You must clearly identify the scenario number you are attempting.

You may use a Spanish dictionary.

Additional space for answers is provided at the end of this booklet.

Use **blue** or **black** ink.

There is a separate answer booklet for Reading. You must complete your answers for Reading in the answer booklet for Reading.

Before leaving the examination room you must give this Directed Writing question and answer booklet and your Reading answer booklet to the Invigilator; if you do not, you may lose all the marks for this paper.

Total marks — 10

Choose **one** of the following two scenarios.

SCENARIO 1: Learning

> You have recently returned from Spain, where you have spent a month attending a Spanish school.
>
> On your return, you have been asked to write an account of your experiences in Spanish to try to encourage other pupils to do the same thing.

You must include the following information and **you should try to add** other relevant details:

- What the school was like **and** how you got on with the other pupils
- What you did while you were there
- How much you understood of the lessons
- What plans you are making to build on the links you made

You should write approximately 120—150 words.

OR

SCENARIO 2: Employability

> Last year, you went with a group of students from your school/college to a town in Spain to study how the tourist industry works. While you were there you had a number of visits.
>
> On your return, you were asked to write a report in Spanish of your visit.

You must include the following information and **you should try to add** other relevant details:

- Where you stayed **and** how you got there
- What you thought of the businesses you visited
- What you learned from the experience
- Whether you would recommend such a visit to others

You should write approximately 120—150 words.

ANSWER SPACE

MARKS | DO NOT WRITE IN THIS MARGIN

Scenario number [   ]

_____

_____

_____

_____

_____

_____

_____

_____

_____

_____

_____

_____

_____

_____

_____

_____

_____

_____

_____

_____

_____

_____

_____

_____

MARKS

ANSWER SPACE (continued)

ANSWER SPACE (continued)

MARKS | DO NOT WRITE IN THIS MARGIN

ANSWER SPACE (continued)

[END OF MODEL QUESTION PAPER]

MARKS

ADDITIONAL SPACE FOR ANSWERS

MARKS

DO NOT WRITE IN THIS MARGIN

ADDITIONAL SPACE FOR ANSWERS

National
Qualifications
MODEL PAPER 1

Spanish
Listening and Writing

Duration — 1 hour

Fill in these boxes and read what is printed below.

Full name of centre

Town

Forename(s)

Surname

Number of seat

Date of birth

Day   Month   Year

Scottish candidate number

Total marks — 30

SECTION 1 — LISTENING — 20 marks

You will hear two items in Spanish. **Before you hear each item, you will have one minute to study the questions.** You will hear each item twice, with an interval of one minute between playings. You will then have time to answer the questions before hearing the next item. Write your answers clearly, in **English**, in the spaces provided.

SECTION 2 — WRITING — 10 marks

Write your answer clearly, in **Spanish**, in the space provided.

Attempt ALL questions. You may use a Spanish dictionary.

Additional space for answers is provided at the end of this booklet. If you use this space you must clearly identify the question number you are attempting.

You are not allowed to leave the examination room until the end of the test.

Use **blue** or **black** ink.

Before leaving the examination room you must give this booklet to the Invigilator; if you do not, you may lose all the marks for this paper.

MARKS DO NOT WRITE IN THIS MARGIN

SECTION 1 — LISTENING — 20 marks
Attempt ALL questions

Item 1

You listen to Maria talking about her summer working in a yoga centre abroad.

(a) How long did Maria work for?   1

_____

(b) Why did she choose to do this work?   1

_____

(c) Maria describes what her daily life was like. What kind of activities did she have to do? Give any **two** details.   2

_____

_____

(d) Maria discusses her hosts while she was in Glasgow.

   (i) Where did she stay while working in Glasgow?   1

_____

   (ii) What problem did this cause at first?   1

_____

(e) Maria discusses her future. What does she have to do now? State any **one** thing.   1

_____

(f) Overall, which statement best describes Maria's opinion about her experiences. Tick (✓) the correct statement.   1

She found it very difficult because the cultures were so different.	
She intends to return to Scotland because she liked it so much.	
Overall, she really enjoyed her experience and hopes others can have a similar one.	

MARKS | DO NOT WRITE IN THIS MARGIN

Item 2

You listen to Mario telling his friend about his stay working on an organic farm (granja ecológica) abroad.

(a) Where exactly has Mario been working?   **1**

_____

(b) When did he return to Spain?   **1**

_____

(c) Mario describes his working week.

   (i) What was his daily routine? Give **two** details.   **2**

_____

_____

   (ii) When was he free?   **1**

_____

   (iii) Why did he not mind getting up when he did? Give any one reason.   **1**

_____

_____

(d) Mario talks about speaking English. How did he get on at first with the language? Give any **two** details.   **2**

_____

_____

(e) Mario talks about the person he became friendly with and what they did.

   (i) What does Mario say about him? Give any **one** detail.   **1**

_____

_____

   (ii) State **any** things he did with his new friend.   **2**

_____

_____

MARKS | DO NOT WRITE IN THIS MARGIN

Item 2 (continued)

(f) State any **one** positive thing he drew from his experience.   **1**

_____

_____

SECTION 2 — WRITING — 10 marks

Mario ha hablado de su verano y de lo que ha hecho. Y tú, ¿qué haces este verano? ¿Tienes un trabajo? ¿Crees que es importante trabajar para los jovenes?

Escribe 120—150 palabras, en español, para expresar tus ideas.

ANSWER SPACE FOR SECTION 2 (continued)

[END OF MODEL QUESTION PAPER]

MARKS DO NOT WRITE IN THIS MARGIN

ADDITIONAL SPACE FOR ANSWERS

MARKS | DO NOT WRITE IN THIS MARGIN

ADDITIONAL SPACE FOR ANSWERS

National Qualifications
MODEL PAPER 1

Spanish
Listening Transcript

Duration — 1 hour

This paper must not be seen by any candidate.

The material overleaf is provided for use in an emergency only (eg the recording or equipment proving faulty) or where permission has been given in advance by SQA for the material to be read to candidates with additional support needs. The material must be read exactly as printed.

Transcript — Higher

Instructions to reader(s):

For each item, read the English **once**, then read the Spanish **twice**, with an interval of 1 minute between the two readings. On completion of the second reading, pause for the length of time indicated in brackets after the item, to allow the candidates to write their answers.

Where special arrangements have been agreed in advance to allow the reading of the material, those sections marked **(f)** should be read by a female speaker and those marked **(m)** by a male; those sections marked **(t)** should be read by the teacher.

(t) Item 1

You listen to Maria talking about her summer working in a yoga centre abroad.

You now have one minute to study the questions for Item 1.

(f) El año pasado estuve trabajando tres meses en una escuela de yoga en Glasgow. Yo practico yoga desde hace siete años y quiero ser profesora de yoga en el futuro. Por eso, Carlos, mi profesor, me ayudó a encontrar trabajo en un centro de yoga en Escocia durante el verano.

Mi trabajo en la escuela era de "chica para todo", es decir, a veces trabajaba en la recepción, contestaba al teléfono, recogía los materiales al final de la clase… ¡De todo, vamos! Lo mejor era que cuando no tenía que trabajar, podía ir gratis a las clases de yoga. Me encantaba porque así podía practicar entre cinco y siete días a la semana.

Durante mi estancia allí, viví en casa de una de las profesoras de la escuela, con su familia. Al principio, no entendía muy bien lo que me decían y creo que ellos también tenían problemas para entenderme a mí. A veces, no era fácil vivir con ellos, porque hay muchas diferencias entre la cultura española y la escocesa. Pero, al final, nos llevamos muy bien y me sentí parte de la familia.

Ahora tengo que terminar mis estudios y seguir practicando y mejorando hasta poder ser yo la profesora, pero en el futuro, cuando tenga mi propia escuela en España, ayudaré a los jóvenes extranjeros que quieran venir a aprender y a trabajar conmigo, para que ellos tengan una experiencia tan positiva como la mía.

(2 minutes)

(t)   Item 2

You listen to Mario telling his friend about his stay working on an organic farm (granja ecológica) abroad.

You now have one minute to study the questions for Item 2.

(f)   ¡Hola, Mario! Hace mucho tiempo que no te veo. ¿Dónde has estado?

(m)   ¡Hola, Carmen! Es verdad que hace mucho tiempo que no nos vemos. He pasado el verano trabajando en una granja ecológica en el norte de Escocia y volví a España el sábado pasado.

(f)   ¿De verdad? ¡Qué interesante! ¿Y cómo era la vida allí?

(m)   En la granja siempre había mucho trabajo. De lunes a sábado, me levantaba a las seis de la mañana, pero tenía libres los domingos, así que podía descansar.

(f)   ¡A las seis de la mañana! ¿Y por qué te tenías que levantar tan temprano?

(m)   Porque había que ocuparse de los animales, por ejemplo, de las vacas. Aunque no me importaba, porque me encanta trabajar con animales y estar en contacto con la naturaleza.

(f)   ¿Y cuánta gente trabajaba en la granja?

(m)   Es una pequeña granja familiar y allí vive toda la familia: un matrimonio con sus tres hijos. Además, hay un chico que vive en el pueblo y que también ayuda en la granja cuando hay más trabajo.

(f)   ¿Y entendías todo lo que te decían?

(m)   Bueno, al principio no entendía casi nada. Me parecía que todos hablaban muy rápido y utilizaban muchas palabras que yo no conocía. Pero todos eran bastante pacientes y me explicaban todo lo que no entendía.

(f)   Me has dicho que los domingos no tenías que trabajar, ¿tenías amigos allí? ¿Y qué hacíais para pasar el tiempo?

(m)   Me hice amigo del hijo mayor del granjero, que tenía un año más que yo. Él me presentó a sus amigos y los fines de semana íbamos de excursión al campo o a nadar. También íbamos al cine que hay en el pueblo de al lado.

(f)   ¡Qué bien! ¿Y no echabas de menos a tu familia y a tus amigos españoles?

(m)   Sí, claro, sobre todo al principio, cuando no conocía a nadie. De todas formas, podía hablar con mi familia y con mis amigos por Internet y por teléfono. ¡Las granjas ecológicas también tienen conexión a Internet!

(f)   Entonces seguro que estás contento y has aprendido mucho, ¿no?

(m)   Sí, muchísimo, ha sido uno de los mejores veranos de mi vida. No solo he aprendido a trabajar con animales, sino que también he mejorado mi inglés y he hecho amigos. ¡Ha sido una experiencia maravillosa!

(2 minutes)

(t)   End of test.

Now look over your answers.

[END OF MODEL TRANSCRIPT]

Page three

Model Paper 2

Whilst this Model Practice Paper has been specially commissioned by Hodder Gibson for use as practice for the Higher (for Curriculum for Excellence) exams, the key reference document remains the SQA Specimen Paper 2014.

HODDER
GIBSON
LEARN MORE

National Qualifications
MODEL PAPER 2

Spanish
Reading

Duration — 1 hour and 40 minutes

Total marks — 30

Attempt ALL questions.

Write your answers clearly, in **English**, in the Reading Answer Booklet provided. In the answer booklet, you must clearly identify the question number you are attempting.

You may use a Spanish dictionary.

Use **blue** or **black** ink.

There is a separate question and answer booklet for Directed Writing. You must complete your answer for Directed Writing in the question and answer booklet for Directed Writing.

Before leaving the examination room you must give your Reading answer booklet and your Directed Writing question and answer booklet to the Invigilator; if you do not, you may lose all the marks for this paper.

Total marks — 30

Read the whole article carefully and then answer, in English, ALL the questions that follow.

The writer discusses music festivals and the people who go to them.

Música y sol, ¿qué más se puede pedir?

Los jóvenes españoles lo tienen muy claro: no hay muchas cosas mejores que pasar tres o cuatro días escuchando música de sus grupos favoritos en directo y disfrutando del buen tiempo. Por eso, el turismo de festivales es perfecto para ellos. Una de las ventajas de los festivales nacionales es el buen tiempo garantizado. Los festivales se celebran en primavera y
5 en verano por todo el país y, en la mayoría de los casos, tanto el público como los artistas disfrutan de las buenas temperaturas y del sol. La lista de festivales españoles de música es larga, aunque cada festival tiene una filosofía y unas características diferentes. No solo se diferencian por el tipo de música que ofrecen, sino también por tener otro tipo de atracciones, como exposiciones de arte contemporáneo, debates y conferencias sobre temas actuales,
10 mercadillos... Así, cada persona elije según sus preferencias.

En general, el público de los festivales de música es gente joven con sus amigos. Los menores de 25 años suelen ser estudiantes universitarios, que se quedan en el camping del festival e intentan no gastar mucho dinero. Este es otro de los atractivos de los festivales nacionales: no hay que comprar billetes de avión, sino que es suficiente con ir en autobús o en coche. En
15 muchos casos, la gente se agrupa y alquilan un autobús que los lleva directamente al festival y después los recoge. Así resulta más barato. En cualquier caso, si estás pensando en asistir a un festival de música, hay algunas cosas que no debes olvidar: en primer lugar... ¡tu entrada! No olvides imprimirla si la has comprado por Internet y meterla en el bolso o la mochila. En segundo lugar, un par de gafas de sol, una gorra o un sombrero, la crema protectora para el sol
20 y una botella grande de agua, porque pasarás mucho tiempo al sol. Si el festival es en primavera o en el norte de España, es buena idea llevar un jersey, porque las temperaturas bajan por la noche. Por último, deja tus problemas en casa y disfruta. Nosotros hemos seleccionado cuatro festivales muy interesantes, dos más famosos y dos todavía independientes, pero de gran calidad:

25 Primavera Sound, que se celebra a finales de mayo en Barcelona, ofrece música independiente de todos los estilos y de grupos y artistas muy diferentes, tanto nacionales como internacionales. Este festival cumplirá quince años en 2016. Este festival es el que más turistas extranjeros recibe. Patrick, un joven alemán, dice: "Me encanta este festival, porque hay grupos muy famosos y muy buen ambiente".

30 El Viña Rock se celebra a finales de abril. Si te gusta el rock, el hip-hop y el reggae, te encantará por su combinación de clásicos del rock español, como Rosendo, con grupos nuevos. En 2012 inauguró el Viña Comedy, una sección del festival dedicada a la comedia y que fue un gran éxito. Ana, fan del festival, dice: "Me encanta la idea de ver comedia y escuchar música rock al mismo tiempo, ¡es la combinación perfecta!"

35 Contempopranea se celebra en Alburquerque y es el festival de música pop independiente favorito de muchos jóvenes. Comparado con los otros festivales, este festival es pequeño, pero de gran calidad. El grupo de música independiente Nieve Polar dice: "Nos gusta venir a tocar aquí cada año, porque nos sentimos como en casa".

El festival Etnosur comenzó en 1997 y tiene música alternativa de todo el mundo y películas,
40 documentales y exposiciones de arte. Fran dice: "Lo mejor para mí son sus cursos: de yoga, danza hawaiana, música brasileña... y los debates sobre temas sociales: es súper completo".

MARKS

Questions

Re-read lines 1—10

1. The opening of the article discusses Spanish music festivals.

    (a) What is one of the advantages festivals in Spain have?   **1**

    (b) Where and when do these festivals take place?   **2**

    (c) What other features do these festivals have? Give **three** details.   **3**

Re-read lines 11—22

2. The author gives some advice to people attending festivals.

    (a) What do we learn about the majority of people who attend these festivals? Give any **three** details.   **3**

    (b) What should you not forget when going to a festival?   **1**

    (c) What might you consider doing if the festival is in the spring? Why?   **2**

Re-read lines 25—34

3. The article gives details of two festivals: Primavera and El Viña Rock.

    (a) How long has Primavera been running?   **1**

    (b) Give **two** details about the recent innovation to El Viña Rock.   **2**

Re-read lines 35—41

4.   The author also discusses two other festivals.

    (a) What makes Etnosur different from other festivals? State **one** thing.   **1**

    (b) What does Fran enjoy doing at Etnosur? Give **two** details.   **2**

5. Now consider the article as a whole. Does the author give the impression that she is positive or negative about music festivals? Give details from the text to justify your answer.   **2**

6. Translate into English:

    "Comparado ... casa." (*lines 36—38*)   **10**

[END OF MODEL QUESTION PAPER]

Page three

National
Qualifications
MODEL PAPER 2

Spanish
Directed Writing

Duration — 1 hour and 40 minutes

Fill in these boxes and read what is printed below.

Full name of centre

Town

Forename(s)

Surname

Number of seat

Date of birth

Day   Month   Year

Scottish candidate number

Total marks — 10

Choose ONE scenario on *Page two* and write your answer clearly, in **Spanish**, in the space provided in this booklet. You must clearly identify the scenario number you are attempting.

You may use a Spanish dictionary.

Additional space for answers is provided at the end of this booklet.

Use **blue** or **black** ink.

There is a separate answer booklet for Reading. You must complete your answers for Reading in the answer booklet for Reading.

Before leaving the examination room you must give this Directed Writing question and answer booklet and your Reading answer booklet to the Invigilator; if you do not, you may lose all the marks for this paper.

Total marks — 10

Choose **one** of the following two scenarios.

SCENARIO 1: Learning

> You have recently returned from Spain, where you have been on a residential Spanish course.
>
> On your return, you have been asked to write an account of your experiences, in Spanish, to to share them with other learners in your school or college.

You must include the following information and **you should try to add** other relevant details:

- Where you went **and** how you got there
- What your daily routine was like
- How you got on with the people you met
- If you would recommend such an experience to others

You should write approximately 120–150 words.

OR

SCENARIO 2: Employability

> Last year, you went to Spain to work in a cafe in a small town. While you were there you stayed with friends of your family.
>
> On your return, you were asked to write a report in Spanish of your visit.

You must include the following information and **you should try to add** other relevant details:

- What the house or flat was like **and** what you thought of the people you were with
- What you did at the cafe
- What you liked/disliked most about the experience
- How you plan to develop the links you made there

You should write approximately 120–150 words.

ANSWER SPACE

Scenario number

_____

_____

_____

_____

_____

_____

_____

_____

_____

_____

_____

_____

_____

_____

_____

_____

_____

_____

_____

_____

_____

_____

_____

_____

MARKS | DO NOT WRITE IN THIS MARGIN

ANSWER SPACE (continued)

MARKS | DO NOT WRITE IN THIS MARGIN

ANSWER SPACE (continued)

MARKS

DO NOT WRITE IN THIS MARGIN

ANSWER SPACE (continued)

[END OF MODEL QUESTION PAPER]

MARKS DO NOT WRITE IN THIS MARGIN

ADDITIONAL SPACE FOR ANSWERS

MARKS | DO NOT WRITE IN THIS MARGIN

ADDITIONAL SPACE FOR ANSWERS

National Qualifications
MODEL PAPER 2

Spanish
Listening and Writing

Duration — 1 hour

Fill in these boxes and read what is printed below.

Full name of centre

Town

Forename(s)

Surname

Number of seat

Date of birth
Day   Month   Year

Scottish candidate number

Total marks — 30

SECTION 1 — LISTENING — 20 marks

You will hear two items in Spanish. **Before you hear each item, you will have one minute to study the questions.** You will hear each item twice, with an interval of one minute between playings. You will then have time to answer the questions before hearing the next item. Write your answers clearly, in **English**, in the spaces provided.

SECTION 2 — WRITING — 10 marks

Write your answer clearly, in **Spanish**, in the space provided.

Attempt ALL questions. You may use a Spanish dictionary.

Additional space for answers is provided at the end of this booklet. If you use this space you must clearly identify the question number you are attempting.

You are not allowed to leave the examination room until the end of the test.

Use **blue** or **black** ink.

Before leaving the examination room you must give this booklet to the Invigilator; if you do not, you may lose all the marks for this paper.

MARKS | DO NOT WRITE IN THIS MARGIN

SECTION 1 — LISTENING — 20 marks

Attempt ALL questions

Item 1

You listen to Sebastian talk about how he uses social networks (redes sociales).

(a) When did Sebastian start using social networks?　　1

_____

(b) His parents were worried at first.

　(i) What were they worried about?　　1

　_____

　(ii) What did he promise them?　　1

　_____

(c) What kind of things did he spend his time online doing at first? State any **two** things.　　2

_____

_____

(d) Sebastian cut down on spending so much time online. State **one** thing he did to achieve this.　　1

(e) What does Sebastian have to do to go to university?　　1

_____

(f) Overall, which statement best describes Sebastian's opinion about using social networks? Tick (✓) the correct statement.　　1

He is aware of the dangers of spending too much time on social networks.	
As he is hard-working, he has no problems combining work and the use of social networks.	
He thinks his use of social networks has gotten out of control.	

MARKS

Item 2

You listen to Esperanza discussing the use of social media by young people.

(a) Who does she say are the most active users of social media?　**1**

_____

(b)　(i) What percentage of young people use at least one social network?　**1**

　　(ii) What does she note about the use of social networks?　**1**

_____

(c) What **two** negative effects does she claim the use of social networks is causing?　**2**

_____

_____

(d) What does she think it is important to do?　**1**

_____

_____

(e) She discusses how to use social media correctly.

　(i) What do we need to learn to do?　**1**

_____

_____

　(ii) What do we forget to do? State any **two** things.　**2**

_____

_____

_____

MARKS | DO NOT WRITE IN THIS MARGIN

Item 2 (continued)

(f) She goes on to talk about the positive aspects of using the internet.

    (i) What does she see as positive and why is this the case? Give **two** details.

      2

_____

_____

    (ii) In which countries is the overuse of social media a particular problem?

      1

_____

_____

MARKS | DO NOT WRITE IN THIS MARGIN

SECTION 2 — WRITING — 10 marks

Esperanza ha hablado de las redes sociales y de lo que hacen los adolescentes. Y tú, ¿utilizas muchas redes sociales y tu movil? ¿Qué haces en tu tiempo libre? ¿Crees que es importante hacer otras cosas en tu tiempo libre?

Escribe 120—150 palabras, en español, para expresar tus ideas.

ANSWER SPACE FOR SECTION 2 (continued)

[END OF MODEL QUESTION PAPER]

ADDITIONAL SPACE FOR ANSWERS

MARKS DO NOT WRITE IN THIS MARGIN

ADDITIONAL SPACE FOR ANSWERS

National Qualifications
MODEL PAPER 2

Spanish
Listening Transcript

Duration — 1 hour

This paper must not be seen by any candidate.

The material overleaf is provided for use in an emergency only (eg the recording or equipment proving faulty) or where permission has been given in advance by SQA for the material to be read to candidates with additional support needs. The material must be read exactly as printed.

HODDER
GIBSON
LEARN MORE

Transcript — Higher

Instructions to reader(s):

For each item, read the English **once**, then read the Spanish **twice**, with an interval of 1 minute between the two readings. On completion of the second reading, pause for the length of time indicated in brackets after the item, to allow the candidates to write their answers.

Where special arrangements have been agreed in advance to allow the reading of the material, those sections marked **(f)** should be read by a female speaker and those marked **(m)** by a male; those sections marked **(t)** should be read by the teacher.

(t)   **Item 1**

You listen to Sebastian talk about how he uses social networks (redes sociales).

You now have one minute to study the questions for Item 1.

(m) El otro día, leí un artículo que decía que uno de los problemas que tenemos los adolescentes es que pasamos demasiado tiempo en Internet, sobre todo en las redes sociales.

Yo empecé a utilizar las redes sociales hace dos años. Al principio, mis padres pensaban que iba a perder el tiempo y que no iba a estudiar, pero yo les prometí que mis notas no cambiarían y, finalmente, me dieron permiso para usarlas.

La verdad es que, durante los dos primeros meses, me pasaba muchísimo tiempo conectado, chateando con mis amigos, compartiendo y comentando fotos... A veces, por la noche, tenía que quedarme haciendo mis deberes hasta muy tarde porque había estado todo el día conectado y no había hecho nada para el instituto. Esto no era muy buena idea, porque al día siguiente, estaba muy cansado en clase.

Finalmente, decidí controlar el tiempo que pasaba conectado: Solo estoy una hora en Internet cuando vuelvo del instituto, y pongo una alarma en mi móvil para asegurarme de estar solamente una hora. Después, si no es muy tarde después de terminar mis deberes, me conecto durante una hora más.

Este año es mi último año de instituto y el año que viene, iré a la Universidad, pero antes de eso tenemos que aprobar los exámenes del instituto, así que este año es un año bastante duro, pero estoy contento de tener mi propio método para no perder demasiado el tiempo.

(2 minutes)

(t)   **Item 2**

You listen to Esperanza discussing the use of social media by young people.

You now have one minute to study the questions for Item 2.

(m)   **Hola, Esperanza. Tú eres experta en nuevas tecnologías y estudias el efecto de las redes sociales en los jóvenes.**

(f)   Sí, las redes sociales son un fenómeno de los últimos años y las utilizan personas de todas las edades. Yo prefiero estudiar las consecuencias que tienen en los jóvenes estudiantes, porque son los más activos en las redes sociales.

(m)   **¿Cuántos jóvenes participan en las redes sociales en nuestro país?**

(f)   En España, el 97% de los adolescentes españoles utilizan al menos una red social. No siempre es la misma red social, sino que cambian. Hay redes que se ponen de moda entre los jóvenes durante un tiempo y después aparecen otras nuevas.

(m)   **¿Cómo afectan las redes sociales a los resultados académicos de los jóvenes?**

(f)   Según nuestros datos, el uso constante de las redes sociales hace que los jóvenes no se concentren tan bien y tengan, en general, peores notas en los exámenes.

(m)   **¿Y cuál es la solución? ¿Prohibir el uso de las redes sociales?**

(f)   No, en absoluto. Las redes sociales tienen muchos aspectos positivos, pero es importante educar a los jóvenes para que las utilicen correctamente.

(m)   **¿Qué significa para ti usarlas correctamente?**

(f)   Para mí, significa saber desconectar. A veces, pensamos que tenemos que estar conectados siempre a una red social, o incluso a muchas, para saber qué pasa a nuestros amigos. Nos concentramos en nuestra vida social por Internet y nos olvidamos de estudiar, hacer los deberes o de pasar tiempo con nuestros amigos y familiares en persona.

(m)   **¿Y cuál es el lado positivo de las redes sociales?**

(f)   Hay muchas ventajas, por ejemplo, nos permiten compartir fotos, ideas, noticias... Para los adolescentes, los amigos son fundamentales y poder compartir cosas con ellos puede ser muy positivo.

(m)   **Se trata de un problema mundial, ¿no?**

(f)   Bueno, es un problema muy moderno, porque antes no había redes sociales, ahora tenemos que educar a los jóvenes para que sean responsables.Es un problema que tenemos en los países desarrollados, porque aquí casi todas las personas tienen acceso a Internet a través del ordenador o del teléfono móvil.

(*2 minutes*)

(t)   **End of test.**

Now look over your answers.

[END OF MODEL TRANSCRIPT]

Model Paper 3

Whilst this Model Practice Paper has been specially commissioned by Hodder Gibson for use as practice for the Higher (for Curriculum for Excellence) exams, the key reference document remains the SQA Specimen Paper 2014.

National
Qualifications
MODEL PAPER 3

Spanish
Reading

Duration — 1 hour and 40 minutes

Total marks — 30

Attempt ALL questions.

Write your answers clearly, in **English**, in the Reading Answer Booklet provided. In the answer booklet, you must clearly identify the question number you are attempting.

You may use a Spanish dictionary.

Use **blue** or **black** ink.

There is a separate question and answer booklet for Directed Writing. You must complete your answer for Directed Writing in the question and answer booklet for Directed Writing.

Before leaving the examination room you must give your Reading answer booklet and your Directed Writing question and answer booklet to the Invigilator; if you do not, you may lose all the marks for this paper.

Total marks — 30

Read the whole article carefully and then answer, in English, ALL the questions that follow.

The writer discusses the brain drain from Spain to Latin America.

Fuga de cerebros españoles a Latinoamérica

Marga tiene 28 años y es arquitecta. Cuando terminó la Universidad trabajó durante seis meses en una empresa en Valencia, pero la empresa donde trabajaba cerró y ella tuvo que buscar trabajo. Desgraciadamente, no fue fácil. Buscó trabajo como arquitecta durante casi un año y, como no lo encontró, buscó trabajo de camarera en bares y cafeterías. "Es muy difícil
5 encontrar trabajo en una cafetería o en un supermercado si has estudiado en la Universidad, porque para esos trabajos prefieren a personas con más experiencia y no tantos estudios", dice Marga. Después de dos años buscando empleo, Marga decidió buscar trabajo en Chile y en dos meses, encontró trabajo como arquitecta en una empresa en Santiago de Chile. Ya lleva un año allí.

10 La historia es muy similar a la de muchos otros jóvenes españoles que han emigrado a Latinoamérica porque no encontraban trabajo después de terminar sus estudios en la Universidad. El sociólogo Pedro Dueñas explica: "Sí, la mayoría de los emigrantes españoles son jóvenes entre 25 y 35 años con estudios universitarios y que no tienen todavía hijos". Francia, el Reino Unido y Alemania son los países que más españoles reciben. Sin embargo,
15 hemos visto que cada vez más españoles viajan a Sudamérica buscando un futuro mejor. En Latinoamérica, los países preferidos son Argentina, Chile, México y Brasil, donde el desempleo es más bajo y existen más oportunidades.

Para muchos, Hispanoamérica es más atractiva por compartir la misma lengua (excepto Brasil) y porque la cultura se parece más a la cultura española que la de los países del norte de
20 Europa. "Aunque tenemos acentos diferentes y a veces no utilizamos las mismas palabras, es maravilloso poder hablar con todo el mundo y entender a la gente", dice Marga. Sin embargo, esto significa que para ver a la familia hay que volar durante diez horas y planear todo con mucho tiempo. "Yo tengo amigos que viven en el Reino Unido y con dos o tres horas de avión, ya están en casa. Si tienen dos o tres de días libres, pueden coger un avión. Yo tengo que
25 planear durante meses y tener suerte, porque a veces los vuelos son demasiado caros", dice Octavio, un joven español que trabaja en Buenos Aires.

En general, estos jóvenes buscan ganar experiencia profesional para así tener más oportunidades de encontrar trabajo en España. No solo quieren mejorar su situación actual, sino que quieren encontrar trabajo en España en el futuro. <u>"Cuando llegué a Buenos Aires,</u>
30 <u>pensé que trabajaría aquí dos años y luego volvería a Mallorca, pero ya han pasado cuatro años y sé que la situación económica en España todavía es muy difícil.</u> Aquí tengo un buen trabajo y también amigos, así que seguiré en Argentina al menos dos años más", dice Octavio. Carlos, ingeniero que vive desde hace un año en México, nos cuenta: "Para mí fue muy duro irme de España, pero sin trabajo no era feliz. México me gusta, pero me gustaría encontrar
35 trabajo en algún país diferente, para conocer más mundo. Por ejemplo, Ecuador o incluso Cuba".

Curiosamente, Cuba se ha convertido en otro de los destinos de los españoles, aunque no es tan fácil conseguir un visado de trabajo* . El caso de Brasil también es interesante, aunque es más difícil encontrar trabajo allí si no se habla portugués, muchos jóvenes españoles buscan
40 trabajo en Brasil mientras estudian la lengua. Las palabras finales las transmite Ana, fisioterapeuta española en Lima: "Disfruto de conocer otra cultura, pero no me gusta que sea una aventura forzada por la crisis en España y me gustaría saber cuándo volveré a casa"

Glossary

Visado de trabajo   working visa

MARKS

Questions

Re-read lines 1—9

1. The opening paragraph talks about Marga's experiences.

    (a) What did she do after graduating? What went wrong there?   2

    (b) Why did she find it difficult to get a job in a cafe or supermarket?   1

    (d) Give **three** details of what she did after being unemployed for two years.   3

Re-read lines 10—17

2. We learn about other possible destinations.

    (a) What attributes do the majority of emigrants share? Mention any **two** things.   2

    (b) Which three countries do most people emigrate to? Give **all three** for the mark.   1

Re-read lines 18—26

3. The article gives more information about reasons for choosing Latin America.

    (a) Why is Latin America so attractive to many young people? Give any **two** reasons.   2

    (b) What is the big difference for people who are in Latin America from those who are in the UK? Give **two** details.   2

Re-read lines 27—34

4. Two other young people, Octavio and Carlo discuss their experiences.

    (a) Why do people want to work abroad?   2

    (b) What made Carlos go to Mexico?   1

Re-read lines 37—42

5. The article reports on two very different destinations. What makes it harder to find work in:

    (a) Cuba   1

    (b) Brazil?   1

6. Now consider the article as a whole. Does the author give the impression that young people are positive or negative about being emigrants? Give details from the text to justify your answer.   **2**

7. Translate into English:

" Cuando ... difícil." (*lines 29—31*)   **10**

[END OF MODEL QUESTION PAPER]

National
Qualifications
MODEL PAPER 3

Spanish
Directed Writing

Duration — 1 hour and 40 minutes

Fill in these boxes and read what is printed below.

Full name of centre

Town

Forename(s)

Surname

Number of seat

Date of birth

Day   Month   Year

Scottish candidate number

Total marks — 10

Choose ONE scenario on *Page two* and write your answer clearly, in **Spanish**, in the space provided in this booklet. You must clearly identify the scenario number you are attempting.

You may use a Spanish dictionary.

Additional space for answers is provided at the end of this booklet.

Use **blue** or **black** ink.

There is a separate answer booklet for Reading. You must complete your answers for Reading in the answer booklet for Reading.

Before leaving the examination room you must give this Directed Writing question and answer booklet and your Reading answer booklet to the Invigilator; if you do not, you may lose all the marks for this paper.

HODDER
GIBSON
LEARN MORE

Total marks — 10

Choose **one** of the following two scenarios.

SCENARIO 1: Society

> You have recently returned from Spain, where you have spent three weeks staying with your Spanish friend.
>
> On your return, you have been asked to write an account of your experiences in Spanish to try to encourage other pupils to do the same thing.

You must include the following information and **you should try to add** other relevant details:

- Where you went **and** how you got there

- What you did while you were there

- How you got on with the family you stayed with

- If you would recommend such an experience to others

You should write approximately 120–150 words.

OR

SCENARIO 2: Culture

> Last summer, you went to Spain to visit a music festival, together with two friends.
>
> On your return, you were asked to write a report in Spanish of your visit.

You must include the following information and **you should try to add** other relevant details:

- Where the festival was **and** what you thought of the music you heard

- What you did apart from listening to music

- How you got on with the people you met there

- How you plan to develop the links you made there

You should write approximately 120–150 words.

ANSWER SPACE

MARKS

DO NOT WRITE IN THIS MARGIN

Scenario number

ANSWER SPACE (continued)

MARKS

ANSWER SPACE (continued)

MARKS DO NOT WRITE IN THIS MARGIN

ANSWER SPACE (continued)

[END OF MODEL QUESTION PAPER]

MARKS

DO NOT
WRITE IN
THIS
MARGIN

ADDITIONAL SPACE FOR ANSWERS

MARKS

ADDITIONAL SPACE FOR ANSWERS

National Qualifications MODEL PAPER 3

Spanish
Listening and Writing

Duration — 1 hour

Fill in these boxes and read what is printed below.

Full name of centre

Town

Forename(s)

Surname

Number of seat

Date of birth

Day	Month	Year

Scottish candidate number

Total marks — 30

SECTION 1 — LISTENING — 20 marks

You will hear two items in Spanish. **Before you hear each item, you will have one minute to study the questions.** You will hear each item twice, with an interval of one minute between playings. You will then have time to answer the questions before hearing the next item. Write your answers clearly, in **English**, in the spaces provided.

SECTION 2 — WRITING — 10 marks

Write your answer clearly, in **Spanish**, in the space provided.

Attempt ALL questions. You may use a Spanish dictionary.

Additional space for answers is provided at the end of this booklet. If you use this space you must clearly identify the question number you are attempting.

You are not allowed to leave the examination room until the end of the test.

Use **blue** or **black** ink.

Before leaving the examination room you must give this booklet to the Invigilator; if you do not, you may lose all the marks for this paper.

SECTION 1 — LISTENING — 20 marks

Attempt ALL questions

Item 1

You listen to Marta who talks about her work as a teacher of Galician in schools in Galicia.

(a) Where exactly does Marta work?   **1**

_____

(b)   (i) Why do her pupils learn through two languages in class?   **1**

_____

    (ii) What does she tell you about how she started speaking Galician? Give **two** details.   **2**

_____

_____

(c) In what way is the teaching split between Spanish and Galician?   **1**

_____

(d) Marta notes two other bilingual regions in Spain. Give **one** of them.   **1**

_____

(e) What sometimes causes problems in her classes?   **1**

_____

(f) Overall, which statement best describes Marta's opinion about the way her school works. Tick (✓) the correct statement.   **1**

She thinks it is difficult to work in two languages.	
The situation in her school is very unusual.	
She thinks the system is very good.	

MARKS | DO NOT WRITE IN THIS MARGIN

Item 2

You listen to Gonzalo who talks about working as an interpreter.

(a) Which **two** languages does he say he works in other than Spanish? 2

_____

_____

(b) Gozalo talks about his clients.

   (i) Who are they, mainly? 1

_____

   (ii) Why is this the case? 1

_____

(c) Why does he not have to interpret between Spanish and Catalan? 1

_____

(d) Gonzalo talks about his private life, when he is not working.

   (i) Who does he talk to in Spanish? 1

_____

   (ii) And who does he talk to in Catalan? 1

_____

(e) Gonzalo discusses the other languages spoken in Spain.

   (i) What are more and more universities doing? 1

_____

   (ii) Does he think it is good that there are several languages in Spain? Why does he think this? 2

_____

_____

_____

MARKS DO NOT WRITE IN THIS MARGIN

Item 2 (continued)

(f) Gonzalo talks about his future plans. What does he intend to do? Give any **two** details.

2

_____

_____

_____

MARKS | DO NOT WRITE IN THIS MARGIN

SECTION 2 — WRITING — 10 marks

Gonzalo ha hablado de los idiomas que habla y de lo que hace con ellos. Y tú, ¿qué idiomas hablas? ¿Te gusta aprender idiomas? ¿Crees que es importante poder comunicarte en varios idiomas?

Escribe 120—150 palabras, en español, para expresar tus ideas.

ANSWER SPACE FOR SECTION 2 (continued)

[END OF MODEL QUESTION PAPER]

ADDITIONAL SPACE FOR ANSWERS

MARKS | DO NOT WRITE IN THIS MARGIN

ADDITIONAL SPACE FOR ANSWERS

National Qualifications
MODEL PAPER 3

Spanish
Listening Transcript

Duration — 1 hour

This paper must not be seen by any candidate.

The material overleaf is provided for use in an emergency only (eg the recording or equipment proving faulty) or where permission has been given in advance by SQA for the material to be read to candidates with additional support needs. The material must be read exactly as printed.

Transcript — Higher

Instructions to reader(s):

For each item, read the English **once**, then read the Spanish **twice**, with an interval of 1 minute between the two readings. On completion of the second reading, pause for the length of time indicated in brackets after the item, to allow the candidates to write their answers.

Where special arrangements have been agreed in advance to allow the reading of the material, those sections marked **(f)** should be read by a female speaker and those marked **(m)** by a male; those sections marked **(t)** should be read by the teacher.

(t) Item 1

You listen to Marta who talks about her work as a teacher of Galician in schools in Galicia.

You now have one minute to study the questions for Item 1.

(m) Trabajo como profesora de gallego en un instituto en un pueblo de Galicia, al noroeste de España. En la región de Galicia los alumnos de las escuelas públicas estudian tanto español como gallego, porque las dos lenguas son lenguas oficiales aquí y es importante que los alumnos conozcan las dos. Yo elegí ser profesora de gallego porque es una lengua muy importante para mí. Mis abuelos hablaban sobre todo en gallego, así que en mi casa nos comunicamos, en general, en gallego, aunque hablamos español si tenemos visitas que no nos entienden.

En los institutos de aquí, los alumnos no solo tienen clases de español y gallego, sino que la mitad de las asignaturas se enseñan en español (por ejemplo, Matemáticas y Física) y la otra mitad en gallego (como, por ejemplo, Geografía e Historia). En mi opinión, esto es esencial para que los alumnos aprendan realmente las dos lenguas y no una más que otra.

Galicia no es la única región de España con dos lenguas oficiales. Cataluña y el País Vasco, por ejemplo, también tienen sus lenguas propias.

La mayoría de mis alumnos son de Galicia, así que no tienen muchos problemas para entender las clases. Sin embargo, tenemos también estudiantes que vienen de otras partes de España y, a veces, es complicado para ellos hablar o entender lo que yo digo. Yo intento ayudarles al máximo y, en mi experiencia, los alumnos aprenden rápidamente y, en general, ellos están contentos de aprender otra lengua.

(2 minutes)

(t) **Item 2**

You listen to Gonzalo who talks about working as an interpreter.

You now have one minute to study the questions for Item 2.

(f) **¡Hola, Gonzalo! ¿Cómo te va el trabajo de intérprete?**

(m) Hola, Nuria. Me va bien, gracias. Últimamente tengo mucho trabajo interpretando y traduciendo catalán, español y alemán, que son los tres idiomas con los que trabajo.

(f) **No sabía que eras intérprete de catalán. ¡Qué interesante! ¿Y quiénes son tus clientes?**

(m) Tengo clientes muy diferentes. Muchos de ellos son hombres de negocios que tienen que viajar y comunicarse con empresas extranjeras. En Cataluña, hay gente que prefiere hablar catalán y no tener que hablar español en sus reuniones de negocios.

(f) **¿Y también tienes que traducir de español a catalán o de catalán a español?**

(m) No, nunca he tenido que hacerlo. Utilizar un intérprete puede ser bastante caro y, en ese caso, la gente se comunica sencillamente en español y no tienen que gastar dinero.

(f) **¿Y cuando no estás trabajando, en qué idioma hablas español o catalán?**

(m) Eso depende. Con mis padres y mis abuelos hablo en español, porque ellos viven en Cataluña, pero son de Andalucía, así que no hablan catalán. Sin embargo, con la familia de mi mujer, hablo en catalán, porque ellos son de Barcelona y prefieren hablar catalán.

(f) **Oye, ¿y hay también intérpretes de las otras lenguas que hay en España, como el vasco o el gallego?**

(m) Sí, claro. Cada vez más universidades preparan a intérpretes de todas las lenguas oficiales que hay en España, no solo de español.

(f) **¿No te parece que es demasiado complicado tener tantas lenguas en un solo país?**

(m) No, al contrario. Creo que es muy importante cuidar y proteger las lenguas que tenemos, porque forman parte de nuestra cultura. Yo quiero que mis hijos sean bilingües y puedan comunicarse igualmente en catalán y en español.

(f) **¿Y piensas estudiar algún otro idioma?**

(m) Sí, ahora estoy perfeccionando mi inglés. Quiero poder trabajar en este idioma, pero para eso es necesario conocer la lengua y la cultura perfectamente.

(f) **Entonces estarás estudiando mucho inglés, ¿no?**

(m) Sí, pero no solo inglés. Los intérpretes tenemos que estar constantemente leyendo y estudiando, porque siempre es posible mejorar en un idioma. Además, tenemos que conocer muy bien la actualidad, no solo de la política o la economía, sino también la cultura, los deportes, etcétera.

(f) **Mucha suerte en tu trabajo y en tus estudios.**

(m) Gracias.

(2 minutes)

(t) **End of test.**

Now look over your answers.

[END OF MODEL TRANSCRIPT]

HIGHER FOR CfE | ANSWER SECTION

SQA AND HODDER GIBSON HIGHER FOR CfE SPANISH 2014

Reading

Question		Expected Answer(s)	Max mark
1		the world we live in now	1
2		the telephone and the internet	1
3		• most people can access all kinds of information • quickly and cheaply	2
4		with the click of a mouse on our computer	1
5		buy food, book a hotel room, read a newspaper, watch tv, communicate with our friends *(any three)*	3
6		• work is becoming more flexible • more and more people are working from home	2
7		people in the third world	1
8		they update the news constantly	1
9		there are no limitations of space /they can include more news	1
10		• some people use the internet to cause harm • they communicate negative ideas • leave negative comments on articles or videos which attack the author • they only want to cause suffering/are never constructive *(any three)*	3
11		• always checking if we have a new email • seeing if someone has left us a message on social media	2
12		He gives a balanced picture: he points out both positive and negative aspects. e.g. • he mentions things we can do • apps and programmes make our life easier • work is easier and faster • poor people in the Third World are disadvantaged • some people abuse the internet (see Qu 10)	2
13		At work a revolution has also taken place/every day in more and more countries/work is getting easier and faster due to numerous programmes / for example, previously you had to write a text on a typewriter (or even by hand)/ photocopy it and send it by letter or fax	2

Directed Writing

Candidates will write a piece of extended writing in Spanish addressing a scenario that has four related bullet points. Candidates must address each bullet point. The first bullet point contains two pieces of information to be addressed. The remaining three bullet points contain one piece of information each. There is a choice of two scenarios and learners must choose one of these.

Mark	Content	Accuracy	Language resource: variety, range, structures
10	• The content is comprehensive • All bullet points are addressed fully and some candidates may also provide additional relevant information	• The language is accurate in all four bullets. However, where the candidate attempts to go beyond the range of the task, a slightly higher number of inaccuracies need not detract from the overall very good impression • A comprehensive range of verbs is used accurately and tenses are consistent and accurate • There is evidence of confident handling of all aspects of grammar and accurate spelling, although the language may contain a number of minor errors, or even one serious error	• The language used is detailed and complex • There is good use of adjectives, adverbs, prepositional phrases and, where appropriate, word order • A comprehensive range of verbs/verb forms, tenses and constructions is used • Some modal verbs and infinitives may be used • The candidate is comfortable with the first person of the verb and generally uses a different verb in each sentence • Sentences are mainly complex and accurate • The language flows well
8	• The content is clear • All bullet points are addressed clearly. The response to one bullet point may be thin, although other bullet points are dealt with in some detail	• The language is mostly accurate. Where the candidate attempts to use detailed and complex language, this may be less successful, although basic structures are used accurately • A range of verbs is used accurately and tenses are generally consistent and accurate • There may be a few errors in spelling, adjective endings and, where relevant, case endings. Use of accents is less secure, where relevant	• The language used is detailed and complex • In one bullet point the language may be more basic than might otherwise be expected at this level • The candidate uses a range of verbs/verb forms and other constructions • There may be less variety in the verbs used • The candidate is comfortable with the first person of the verb and generally uses a different verb in each sentence • Sentences are generally complex and mainly accurate • Overall the writing will be very competent, essentially correct, but may be pedestrian

Mark	Content	Accuracy	Language resource: variety, range, structures
6	• The content is adequate and may be similar to that of an 8 • Bullet points may be addressed adequately, however one of the bullet points may not be addressed	• The language may be mostly accurate in two or three bullet points. However, in the remaining one or two, control of the language structure may deteriorate significantly • The verbs are generally correct, but basic • Tenses may be inconsistent, with present tenses being used at times instead of past tenses • There may be errors in spelling, adjective endings and some prepositions may be inaccurate or omitted. There are quite a few errors in other parts of speech – personal pronouns, gender of nouns, adjective endings, cases (where relevant), singular/plural confusion – and in the use of accents (where relevant) • Overall, there is more correct than incorrect and there is the impression that the candidate can handle tenses	• There are some examples of detailed and complex language • The language is perhaps repetitive and uses a limited range of verbs and fixed phrases not appropriate to this level • The candidate relies on a limited range of vocabulary and structures • There is minimal use of adjectives, probably mainly after "is" • The candidate has a limited knowledge of plurals • A limited range of verbs is used to address some of the bullet points • The candidate copes with the past tense of some verbs • When using the perfect tense, the past participle is incorrect or the auxiliary verb is omitted on occasion • Sentences are mainly single clause and may be brief
4	• The content may be limited and the Directed Writing may be presented as a single paragraph • Bullet points may be addressed in a limited way or • **Two** of the bullet points are not be addressed	• The language is mainly inaccurate and after the first bullet the control of the language structure may deteriorate significantly. • A limited range of verbs is used • Ability to form tenses is inconsistent • In the use of the perfect tense the auxiliary verb is omitted on a number of occasions • There may be confusion between the singular and plural form of verbs • There are errors in many other parts of speech – gender of nouns, cases, singular/plural confusion – and in spelling and, where appropriate, word order • Several errors are serious, perhaps showing mother tongue interference	• There is limited use of detailed and complex language • The language is repetitive, with undue reliance on fixed phrases and a limited range of common basic verbs such as to be, to have, to play, to watch • The candidate mainly copes only with simple language • The verbs "was" and "went" may also be used correctly • Sentences are basic and there may be one sentence that is not intelligible to a sympathetic native speaker • An English word may appear in the writing or a word may be omitted • There may be an example of serious dictionary misuse
2	• The content may be basic or similar to that of a 4 or even a 6 • Bullet points are addressed with difficulty.	• The language is inaccurate in all four bullets and there is little control of language structure • Many of the verbs are incorrect or even omitted. There is little evidence of tense control • There are many errors in other parts of speech — personal pronouns, gender of nouns, cases, singular/plural confusion, prepositions, for instance	• There is little use, if any, of detailed and complex language • Verbs used more than once may be written differently on each occasion . • The candidate displays almost no knowledge of the past tense of verbs • The candidate cannot cope with more than one or two basic verbs • Sentences are very short and some sentences may not be understood by a sympathetic native speaker

Mark	Content	Accuracy	Language resource: variety, range, structures
0	• The content is very basic • The candidate is unable to address the bullet points Or • **Three** or more of the bullet points are not be addressed	• The language is seriously inaccurate in all four bullets and there is almost no control of language structure • Most errors are serious • Virtually nothing is correct • Very little is intelligible to a sympathetic native speaker	• There is no evidence of detailed and complex language • The candidate may only cope with the verbs to have and to be • There may be several examples of mother tongue interference. • English words are used • Very few words are written correctly in the modern language. • There may be several examples of serious dictionary misuse

Section 1 — Listening

Item 1

Question			Expected Answer(s)
1	a	i	• He had problems with his knee
1	a	ii	• He has a season ticket/is a supporter of his favourite team • He never misses his favourite team's games/matches • He is an assistant coach for a team of small children *Any one of the above 3 points for 1 mark*
1	b		• At five he played the guitar. • At school he wrote songs
1	c		• A form of expressing himself • A way of forgetting his problems *Any one of the above 2 points for 1 mark*
1	d	i	• (To participate in) team sports • (To participate in) social networks
1	d	ii	• Young people spend more time communicating via social networks than face to face.
1	e		• Leisure activities are really important to him.

Item 2

Question			Expected Answer(s)
2	a		• She started singing on her (white) sofa at home • Posting her videos on social networks • New technologies were very important *Any two of the above points for 2 marks*
2	b		• She doesn't care/it does not matter/she doesn't care at all • Her job is to sing/play the guitar/write songs *Any one of the above points for 1 mark*
2	c	i	• If they recognise her in a restaurant, she gets one of the best/better tables • In the streets people smile at her • Fans ask for her autograph *Any one of the above points for 1 mark*
2	c	ii	• It is difficult to escape • It is difficult not to draw attention to herself • She would like to walk into a shop where the shop attendants did not recognise her *Any one of the above points for 1 mark*

Question			Expected Answer(s)
2	d	i	• Going on holiday • Relaxing on the beach *Any one of the above points for 1 mark*
2	d	ii	• Because she misses her mother's cooking/food • Because she likes to spend time with her family *Any one of the above points for 1 mark*
2	e		• Walking on the beach • Exercising in the gym • Going to a zumba class *Any one of the above points for 1 mark*
2	f		• Has never smoked • Balanced diet • Doesn't eat much fat/fatty food • Tries to sleep for 8 hours *Any two of the above points for 2 marks*
2	g		• She speaks French fluently • She always sings one song in French at her concerts • She wants to improve her English because she thinks languages are important • She likes listening to music in English *Any two of the above points for 2 marks*

Section 2 — Writing

Candidates will write 120—150 words in a piece of extended writing in Spanish addressing a stimulus of three questions in Spanish.

Mark	Content	Accuracy	Language resource: variety, range, structures
10	• The content is comprehensive • The topic is addressed fully, in a balanced way • Some candidates may also provide additional information. • Overall this comes over as a competent, well thought-out response to the task which reads naturally.	• The language is accurate throughout. However where the candidate attempts to go beyond the range of the task, a slightly higher number of inaccuracies need not detract from the overall very good impression • A comprehensive range of verbs is used accurately and tenses are consistent and accurate • There is evidence of confident handling of all aspects of grammar and spelling accurately, although the language may contain a number of minor errors, or even one serious major error	• The language used is detailed and complex • There is good use of adjectives, adverbs, prepositional phrases and, where appropriate, word order. • A comprehensive range of verbs/verb forms, tenses and constructions is used. • Some modal verbs and infinitives may be used. • The candidate is comfortable with the first person of the verb and generally uses a different verb in each sentence. • The candidate uses co-ordinating conjunctions and subordinate clauses throughout the writing. • Sentences are mainly complex and accurate. • The language flows well
8	• The content is clear • The topic is addressed clearly	• The language is mostly accurate. However where the candidate attempts to use detailed and complex language, this may be less successful, although basic structures are used accurately • A range of verbs is used accurately and tenses are generally consistent and accurate • There may be a few errors in spelling, adjective endings and, where relevant, case endings. Use of accents is less secure. • Verbs and other parts of speech are used accurately but simply.	The language used is detailed and complex • The candidate uses a range of verbs/verb forms and other constructions. • There may be less variety in the verbs used. • The candidate is comfortable with the first person of the verb and generally uses a different verb in each sentence. • Most of the more complex sentences use co-ordinating conjunctions, and there may also be examples of subordinating conjunctions where appropriate. • Sentences are generally complex and mainly accurate. • At times the language may be more basic than might otherwise be expected at this level. • There may be an example of minor misuse of dictionary. • Overall the writing will be very competent, essentially correct, but may be pedestrian.

Mark	Content	Accuracy	Language resource: variety, range, structures
6	• The content is adequate and may be similar to that of an 8 or a 10 • The topic is addressed adequately	• The language may be mostly accurate. However, in places, control of the language structure may deteriorate significantly. • The verbs are generally correct, but basic. Tenses may be inconsistent, with present tenses being used at times instead of past tenses. • There may be errors in spelling, e.g. reversal of vowel combinations adjective endings and some prepositions may be inaccurate or omitted, e.g. I went the town. There are quite a few errors in other parts of speech – personal pronouns, gender of nouns, adjective endings, cases, singular/plural confusion – and in the use of accents • Overall, there is more correct than incorrect and there is the impression that the candidate can handle tenses	• There are some examples of detailed and complex language • The language is perhaps repetitive and uses a limited range of verbs and fixed phrases not appropriate to this level. • The candidate relies on a limited range of vocabulary and structures. • There is minimal use of adjectives, probably mainly after "is". • The candidate has a limited knowledge of plurals. • The candidate copes with the present tense of most verbs. • Where the candidate attempts constructions with modal verbs, these are not always successful. • Sentences are mainly single clause and may be brief • There may be some misuse of dictionary
4	• The content may be limited and may be presented as a single paragraph • The topic is addressed in a limited way	• The language used to address the more predictable aspects of the task may be accurate. However, major errors occur when the candidate attempts to address a less predictable aspect. • A limited range of verbs is used. • Ability to form tenses is inconsistent. • In the use of the perfect tense the auxiliary verb is omitted on a number of occasions. • There may be confusion between the singular and plural form of verbs. • There are errors in many other parts of speech – gender of nouns, cases, singular/plural confusion – and in spelling and, where appropriate, word order. • Several errors are serious, perhaps showing mother tongue interference. • Overall there is more incorrect than correct.	• There is limited use of detailed and complex language and the language is mainly simple and predictable • The language is repetitive, with undue reliance on fixed phrases and a limited range of common basic verbs such as to be, to have, to play, to watch. • There is inconsistency in the use of various expressions, especially verbs. • Sentences are basic and there may be one sentence that is not intelligible to a sympathetic native speaker. • An English word may appear in the writing or a word may be omitted. • There may be an example of serious dictionary misuse.
2	• The content may be basic or similar to that of a 4 or even a 6 • The topic is thinly addressed	• The language is almost completely inaccurate throughout the writing and there is little control of language structure • Many of the verbs are incorrect or even omitted. There is little evidence of tense control. • There are many errors in other parts of speech — personal pronouns, gender of nouns, cases, singular/plural confusion • Prepositions are not used correctly.	• There is little use, if any, of detailed and complex language • The candidate has a very limited vocabulary. • Verbs used more than once may be written differently on each occasion. • The candidate cannot cope with more than one or two basic verbs. • Sentences are very short and some sentences may not be understood by a sympathetic native speaker • Several English or "made-up" words may appear in the writing. • There are examples of serious dictionary misuse.

Mark	Content	Accuracy	Language resource: variety, range, structures
0	• The content is very basic. • The candidate is unable to address the topic.	• The language is seriously inaccurate throughout the writing and there is almost no control of language structure • (Virtually) nothing is correct. • Most of the errors are serious. • Very little is intelligible to a sympathetic native speaker.	• There is no evidence of detailed and complex language • The candidate copes only with "have" and "am". • There may be several examples of mother tongue interference. • Very few words are written correctly in the modern language. • English words are used. • There may be several examples of serious dictionary misuse.

HIGHER FOR CfE SPANISH
MODEL PAPER 1

Reading

Question		Expected Answer(s)	Max mark
1	a	• Physical bullying has not got worse, but there is more psychological (mental) bullying	1
	b	• Young people are using new technology to bully • Especially on social networks • They are using social networks to laugh at/make fun of victims *Any 2 of the above points for a maximum of 2 marks*	2
	c	• They encourage other people to join in online	1
2	a	• A classmate started bullying him on his social network • Leaving threatening or insulting messages	2
	b	• Pedro dropped him as a friend • He then opened a new account in Pedro's name • And used it to insult him and insult others in Pedro's name *Any 2 of the above points for a maximum of 2 marks*	2
	c	• Bullies used to bully people they knew personally • Now it can be people in different schools they do not actually know *Any 1 of the above points for a maximum of 1 mark*	1
3	a	• Doing or saying things which are different • Someone always reading comics • Someone wearing very different clothes *Any 2 of the above points for a maximum of 2 marks*	2
	b	• His mother thought he should lose weight to stop being bullied • His teacher said it was the bullies who had to change, not him	2
4		• It is easier to prove bullying (you can find out which computer the messages are written from) • The guilty can be blamed (punished) or • re-educated to understand the negative effects their actions have on someone's life	2
5	a	• They organise classes (courses) • Psychologists or teachers explain what bullying is • And what to do if you are suffering from it or know a victim *Any 2 of the above points for a maximum of 2 marks*	2

Question		Expected Answer(s)	Max mark
	b	• Take action or invite young sufferers to talk about it with parents and teachers	1
6		Outline of posible answers: No, the author thinks it is a problem that can be dealt with for the following reasons: • Only 11% of young people are being bullied • He explains that part of the problem is parents and teachers doing the wrong thing • Pedro's teacher explained how it should stop • Leticia Campos explains we should not blame the victim • The way it is easy to find evidence of cyber bullying is shown • Tracing, punishing and re-educating bullies is discussed • Examples are given of what schools are doing to address the problem • It is explained at the end what we need to do next	2
7		Este tipo de acoso causa más dolor y trauma para las víctimas **This kind of bullying causes more trauma and pain for the victims** porque en muchos casos es de una humillación pública **because in many cases it is a public humiliation** A veces, son acosados **Sometimes they have been bullied** por personas que no conocen **by people they do not know** pero que han visto sus fotos en las redes sociales **but who have seen their photos on social networks.**	10

Directed Writing

Please refer back to p114–116 for further advice on the General Marking Principles for Directed Writing.

Section 1 — Listening

Item 1

Question			Expected Answer(s)	Max mark
1	a		• Three months	1
1	b		• She wants to be a yoga teacher	1
1	c		• Work in reception • Answer the phone • Tidy away the material *Any two of the above 3 points for 2 marks*	2
1	d	i	• With one of the teachers	1

Question			Expected Answer(s)	Max mark
1	d	ii	• She could not understand what they were saying to her • They had problems understanding her • They had problems understanding each other *Any one of the above 3 points for 1 mark*	1
1	e		• Finish her studies • Keep practising/improving to become a teacher *Any one of the above 2 points for 1 mark*	1
1	f		• Overall, she really enjoyed her experience and hopes others can have a similar one.	1

Item 2

Question			Expected Answer(s)	Max mark
2	a		• The north of Scotland	1
2	b		• Last Saturday	1
2	c	i	• From Monday to Saturday • He got up at 6am	2
2	c	ii	• Sunday	1
2	c	iii	• He liked working with the animals • Liked being in touch with nature *Any one of the above 2 points for 1 mark*	1
2	d		• At first he understood almost nothing • They spoke fast and used words he didn't know • They were patient and explained things *Any two of the above points for 2 marks*	2
2	e	i	• The oldest son of the family • He was a year older than Mario *Any one of the above 2 points for 1 mark*	1
2	e	ii	• He introduced Mario to his friends • They went on excursions at the weekend • They went to the cinema in the next town/village *Any two of the above points for 2 marks*	2
2	f		• He learned to work with animals • Improved his English • Made friends *Any one of the above points for 1 mark*	1

Section 2 — Writing

Please see p117–119 for General Marking Principles for Writing.

HIGHER FOR CfE SPANISH MODEL PAPER 2

Reading

Question		Expected Answer(s)	Max mark
1	a	• Good weather is guaranteed	1
	b	• All over the country • In spring **and** summer	2
	c	• Art exhibitions • Debates and conferences • Markets	3
2	a	• Under 25 • University students • Stay on the festival campus • Don't intend to spend much money *Any 3 of above points for a maximum of 3 marks*	3
	b	• Your entry ticket	1
	c	• Taking a pullover • Temperatures drop at night	2
3	a	• It will have been running for 15 years in 2016	1
	b	• A section of the festival was dedicated to comedy • It was a great success	2
4	a	• It has films and documentaries • It has art exhibiting *Any of the above points for 1 mark*	2
	b	• Going to courses such as (yoga, Hawaiian dance, Brazilian music) any example • Taking part in debates on social issues	2
5		Outline of possible answers: The author is positive about festivals for the following reasons: — In the first sentence she describes the pleasures of going to a festival — She talks about enjoying the sun and nice temperatures — She describes the variety of different festivals you can go to — She talks about leaving your problems at home and enjoying yourself — The festivals selected are said to be of great quality — She says you will be delighted with Viña Rock	2

Question			Expected Answer(s)	Max mark
6			Comparado con los otros festivales/ este festival es pequeño, pero de gran calidad. **Compared with the other festivals/this festival is small but of high quality.** El grupo de música independiente Nieve Polar dice: **The indie music band Nieve Polar says:** Nos gusta venir a tocar aquí cada año, **we like coming to play here every year** porque nos sentimos como en casa. **because we feel as if we are at home.**	10

Directed Writing

Please refer back to p114–116 for further advice on the General Marking Principles for Directed Writing.

Section 1 — Listening

Item 1

Question			Expected Answer(s)	Max mark
1	a		• Two years ago	1
1	b	i	• He would waste time/not study	1
1	b	ii	• His marks would not change (get worse)	1
1	c		• Chatting with his friends • Sharing/discussing photos	2
1	d		• He limited himself to an hour (after school) • He set an alarm to limit his time *Any one of the above 2 points for 1 mark*	1
1	e		• Pass his exams	1
1	f		• He is aware of the dangers of spending too much time on social networks	1

Item 2

Question			Expected Answer(s)	Max mark
2	a		• Young students	1
2	b	i	• 97%	1
2	b	ii	• People change the ones they use, there are fashions	1
2	c		• Young people do not concentrate as well • They have worse marks in exams	2
2	d		• Teach young people to use them properly	1
2	e	i	• To switch off (disconnect)	1

Question			Expected Answer(s)	Max mark
2	e	ii	• Study • Do homework • Spend time with our friends and families *Any two of the above points for 2 marks*	2
2	f	i	• They can share photos, ideas, • Their friends are very important (fundamental) • It is very positive to be able to share with friends *Any two of the above points for 2 marks*	2
2	f	ii	• Developed countries	1

Section 2 — Writing

Please see p117–119 for General Marking Principles for Writing.

HIGHER FOR CfE SPANISH
MODEL PAPER 3

Reading

Question		Expected Answer(s)	Max mark
1	a	• She worked for six months for a company in Valencia • The firm closed and she had to look for another job	2
	b	• It is difficult to find such a job if you have been to university • Employers prefer someone with more experience and less qualifications *Any 1 of above points for a maximum of 1 mark*	1
	c	• She decided to look for work in Chile • She found a job in two months • She is working as an architect • She has been there a year already *Any 3 of above points for a maximum of 3 marks*	3
2	a	• They are between 25 and 35 • They have degrees • They have no children *Any 2 of above points for a maximum of 2 marks*	2
	b	• France, UK and Germany (all three for the mark)	1
3	a	• They share the same language (other than Brazil) • The culture is closer to Spain than the culture of Northern Europe • Although they have different accents they understand each other *Any 2 of above points for a maximum of 2 marks*	2
	b	• From Latin America it is a ten hour flight and you have to plan well in advance • From the UK it is two or three hours by plane, and you can go home if you have a couple of days off	2
4	a	• To gain professional experience • It will be easier to find a job when they return to Spain in the future	2
	b	• He had no work and was unhappy	1
5	a	• It is not easy to get a work permit	1
	b	• It is harder to get a job if you don't speak Portuguese	1

Question	Expected Answer(s)	Max mark
6	Outline of possible answers: The author gives the impression that the young people are positive on the whole, and sees the advantages of what they are doing, for the following reasons: • Marga was unhappy looking for work in Spain and found work quickly in Chile. She has been there a year • Young people are said to be looking for "a better future" • Marga says how marvellous it is to be able to talk the same language • The young people are looking to improve their employment prospects through gaining experience • Octavio has a good job and friends, and intends to spend another two years there • Carlos says he is happy in Mexico • Ana says she is happy to know a different culture	2
7	Cuando llegué a Buenos Aires **When I arrived in Buenos Aires** pensé que trabajaría aquí dos años **I thought I would work here for two years** y luego volvería a Mallorca **and then (I would) return to Majorca** pero ya han pasado cuatro años **but four years have passed already** y sé que la situación económica en España todavía es muy difícil **and I know the economic situation in Spain is still very difficult.**	10

Directed Writing

Please refer back to p114–116 for further advice on the General Marking Principles for Directed Writing.

Section 1 — Listening

Item 1

Question			Expected Answer(s)	Max mark
1	a		• School in Galicia in northwest Spain	1
1	b	i	• They are both official languages	1
1	b	ii	• Her grandparents only spoke in Galician • In her house they normally spoke Galician • They only spoke Spanish if they had visitors who did not understand Galician *Any two of above 3 points for 2 marks*	2
1	c		• Half and half (half the subjects are taught in each language)	1
1	d		• Catalonia or the Basque country	1
1	e		• When students from other parts of Spain come to the school	1
1	f		• She thinks the system is very good	1

Item 2

Question			Expected Answer(s)	Max mark
2	a		• Catalan • German	2
2	b	i	• Businessmen	1
2	b	ii	• Some people prefer to speak Catalan and not Spanish in business meetings	1
2	c		• It is expensive to hire an interpreter, so they communicate in Spanish	1
2	d	i	• His parents and grandparents	1
2	d	ii	• His wife's family	1
2	e	i	• Training interpreters in all of Spain's languages	1
2	e	ii	• Yes he thinks it is important to look after/protect them • They are part of Spanish culture	2
2	f		• Improve his English • (Know its language and culture perfectly) • Keep up to date with politics and economics *Any two of above points for 2 marks*	2

Section 2 — Writing

Please see p117—119 for General Marking Principles for Writing.

Acknowledgements

Hodder Gibson would like to thank SQA for use of any past exam questions that may have been used in model papers, whether amended or in original form.